Henry Day

From the Pyrenees to the Pillars of Hercules

Observations on Spain, its history and its people

Henry Day

From the Pyrenees to the Pillars of Hercules
Observations on Spain, its history and its people

ISBN/EAN: 9783337239749

Printed in Europe, USA, Canada, Australia, Japan

Cover: Foto ©ninafisch / pixelio.de

More available books at **www.hansebooks.com**

FROM THE

PYRENEES

TO THE

PILLARS OF HERCULES

OBSERVATIONS ON SPAIN

ITS HISTORY AND ITS PEOPLE

BY

HENRY D<!-- obscured -->

AUTHOR OF "THE LAWYER<!-- obscured -->"

NEW YORK

G. P. PUTNAM'S S<!-- obscured -->

27 AND 29 WEST TWENTY-THIRD <!-- obscured -->

1883

PREFACE.

Books of travel can claim little originality so far as they state facts. These are not manufactured, but gathered from all sources at command, from history, from oral communications, and not least from guide-books. We wish to acknowledge our obligations to Ford's Book on Spain, which is one of the most thorough and reliable books on that country, and a most complete guide to the traveler. We have not scrupled to use the facts collated by him with the utmost freedom.

It may be asked why should any one presume to write a book on a subject so often treated by others. The answer is that no two persons are apt to notice precisely the same objects in traveling, or if they do, they see them with different degrees of interest and in different combinations. One traveler may notice natural objects, the geography and topography of the country. He may be fond of nature. Another will be more interested in the artificial characteristics of the cities, the architecture, the arts. Another will turn his attention more to the people, their education, manners, dress, amusements, and their social life. Another will notice all objects and people in the light of history.

There is a great variety in all these subjects and an infinite variety in the way of stating and combining them, so that a number of books may be written on the same country by different persons, and all have the freshness of originality, while the general framework of facts is common to all. So much we are bound to say, as apology for writing on a trite subject. As the qualities of writers differ, so the taste of readers differ, so that all writers, however humble their pretensions, may find some sympathetic readers. With this hope, this humble effort is dedicated to the Readers by

THE AUTHOR.

CONTENTS.

	PAGE
PRELIMINARY OBSERVATIONS ON THE CHARACTER OF THE COUNTRY AND THE PEOPLE	1
BARCELONA	28
MONSERRAT	35
BARCELONA TO MADRID	44
MADRID	47
TOLEDO	105
LA MANCHA	120
CADIZ	178
GIBRALTAR AND CONSTANTINOPLE	188
TANGIER	205
MOROCCO	210
MALAGA	214
MADRID TO BAYONNE	223
BURGOS	227
THE PYRENEES	235

FROM THE PYRENEES TO THE PILLARS OF . HERCULES.

PRELIMINARY OBSERVATIONS ON THE CHARACTER OF THE COUNTRY AND THE PEOPLE.

SPAIN lies out of the ordinary route of travel. Less is known of it than of any other European State. It has a wonderful history, which has never been well written by English authors.

By looking at the map of Europe, some of the geographical peculiarities of the Spanish Peninsula will be seen, and these should be noted. It reaches a more southern latitude than any other part of Europe. Cadiz and Malaga lie as far south as Tunis, and have an African climate and productions. Washed by the waters of the Bay of Biscay, the Atlantic and the Mediterranean, it is almost an island, having a coast line of about 2,500 miles.

It lays one hand on the Straits of Gibraltar, the grand highway of commerce to the Orient, while her left hand holds the Pyrenees as her impregnable fortress.

Thus by nature she is constituted an independent

kingdom, with unrivaled commercial facilities, with climate and productions entirely unique on the continent of Europe. She has an area of about 175,000 square miles, or one nearly equal to France, four times as large as the State of New York, and about twice as large as the British Isles. She has a population of about sixteen and one-half millions, while France has about thirty-six millions.

The central part of Spain lies on a high plateau from two to three thousand feet above the sea, and this is reached generally by traveling sixty or eighty miles back from the coast.

There are seven distinct chains of mountains in Spain, with a general dip toward the west.

Along the plains and valleys, between these chains run the six principal rivers, all, excepting the Ebro, emptying into the Atlantic.

Most of them, being rapid mountain streams, are of no great use for commercial purposes, excepting the Tagus and Duero, the mouths of which belong to Portugal. There is no internal communication in Spain by means of rivers. The variety of altitude gives great variety of climate and productions; you are everywhere within view of mountains; the highest, the Sierra Morena and Sierra Nevada, are constantly covered with snow.

The high central table-lands out of which these mountains rise comprise about one-half of the land of the kingdom. They are denuded of trees, except where the olive groves abound in the southern part. Cold, damp and wind-rent in winter, they are burned up by drought in summer. Want of water is the great curse to this part of Spain. The average rainfall during the year at Madrid, the centre of this plateau, is only twelve inches, while the average temperature is 65° Fahrenheit, and often ranging in the summer months from 100° to 110°. Here are no fields of grass; but the soil, where it is irrigated, or when the season has sufficient rain, produces excellent grain of different varieties. The narrower valleys, which can be watered from the snows melting on the mountains, and the strip of land along the coast, especially on the east and south sides, are in perfect contrast to the bare plains of the interior.

Shielded in winter by the high mountains from the northern blasts, fanned in spring and autumn by the breezes of the Mediterranean, and watered in summer by the melting snows of the Sierras, they present a picture of a perfect earthly paradise. No wonder the Moors, from the hot deserts of Africa and the level, sterile wastes of Arabia, glowed with delight as their eyes rested on these charming valleys. No wonder they fought to obtain them, and periled their all to keep them. Here they found the orange, the fig, the aloe, the pomegranate, the grape and the palm, the almond and the sugar cane, the mulberry and the cotton tree, the citron and the olive, all growing side by side. Here was perpetual spring.

Spain is not deficient in mineral resources. She has coal, iron, copper, marbles of all kinds, gold and silver; but she has not the enterprise to develop them. The gold of the New World demoralized them centuries ago. It led them to despise labor and commerce. When the gold of the New World no longer flowed in upon them, they sank, a poverty-stricken people, and have never learned the art of self-support.

There is great variety of climate in Spain, arising from difference in altitude. Among the mountains of Grenada and the Pyrenees the weather is delightful, even in summer. Along the coast the heat of summer is generally very great, but warm and spring-like all winter, when the grain is green, the oranges ripening, and roses blooming. The houses of the people have no fire-places.

To one accustomed to our warm houses they seem chilly in midwinter in Madrid and Grenada, which have an altitude of 2,500 feet.

When it is particularly cold the people have a pan of charcoal, called a brazier, set on the floor, in a wooden frame, which gives out a gentle heat for a long time, enabling them to keep the feet warm and tempering the chilliness of the room. The poor people have no such luxury, even, as this. In the lower stories of their stone houses the dampness and cold are penetrating, and you will see the people in the houses wrapped in cloaks. Little children look chilled, and nothing is more common than to hear an ominous cough, showing that pulmonary diseases prevail. As the hot season is the longest and severest, the houses and streets are built with reference to keeping out the heat of summer. The people depend on the sun, in winter, for warmth. You will often see women and children ranged along by a wall in the sun, much as we would gather around a fire. There is often a difference of 30 or 40 degrees between the sunny and the shady side of the street. The weather in Barcelona, Valencia, Malaga and Gibraltar is charming in winter; even invalids would find very few days when fire is needed.

It hardly seemed possible to us, in January, when the sun was too warm in the middle of the day, and trees in bloom, that there could be, in the same latitude in America, snow and ice, and the dreariness of winter.

Formerly there were fourteen different political divisions in Spain, more or less independent of each other, such as Leon, Navarre, the two Castiles, Catalonia, Estremadura, Andalusia, Grenada, etc., having different rulers and different laws, and hence, in many respects, the people of these different provinces differ in character, manners, customs, dress and language.

The Castiles embrace the largest and the central portion of Spain. They were so named from the number of their castles in olden times. Never being thoroughly subdued by the Moors, always loyal to the Church, its great champion against the Moslem invader, they are the stern, haughty, sedate aristocracy of all Spain, the descendants of the old Goths, of the famous old knights and warriors who, under Ferdinand and Isabella, expelled the Moors, who despise labor and trade, who live on their high plains and lonely steppes, which are treeless and songless, without hamlets or fences, where every height is surmounted by some decaying castle, around and in which deeds of high valor have been done by their ancestors, and which are perpetuated among them in romance and song. They cling to their gloomy, joyless plains with all the devotion of ancient chivalry.

The Catalans, in the northeast part of Spain, are more industrious, active and commercial in their habits. They are called the Yankees of Spain, and have been merchants from the days of the Phœnicians. Andalusia, in the southwestern part, is the garden of Spain. It embraces Cordova, Seville, Cadiz and Gibraltar. The people are mercurial, happy and easy-going, more fond of pleasure, and of social and intellectual pursuits, than of labor. They have more of the manners, customs, character and blood of the Moors than the Castilians. Nature is so prodigal, the climate so benignant, that the least labor supports life. A little oil, garlic, bread and oranges are all that the peasant requires. The sun and his cloak warm him in winter; his tall house and open court shade him in summer. Here originated some of the finest scholars and the best artists of Spain. One cannot fail, in the easy life, the procrastination of all activity, the everlasting to-morrow, the songs, the guttural accent, the dress and the houses, to see the resemblance to the Arab race.

Estremadura, in the western part, is almost a desert, although one of the best-watered and most fertile provinces. It is given up to immense herds of swine and sheep. It was once highly cultivated, and well populated by the Moors, but when they were expelled it was abandoned to wild birds and beasts for ages, until gradually the shepherds of Leon and the northern provinces brought down their flocks in winter, to feed on these unclaimed pastures, until at length they claimed the prescriptive right of pasturage in summer, which begat infinite disputes between them and the residents. This right at last settled into a law called the Custom of Mesta. These flocks would come in detachments of 10,000, each having a conductor, fifty attendants, and fifty dogs. Some of the flocks would travel 500 miles. By the law of the Mesta a sheep-walk of ninety paces broad was left uninclosed for the driving and feeding of the sheep, which prevented all proper cultivation. Here were born and reared the wild and bloody men, Cortez and Pizarro.

Ronda and Grenada, to the southeast, are mountainous provinces, with beautiful fertile valleys, called vegas, watered from the snows of the surrounding mountains. They are, under the influence of irrigation, marvels of fertility, sometimes producing four crops, and never less than two, annually.

They were the strongholds of the Moors, and the last from which they were dislodged. They held on to these mountain-locked valleys and to these fortresses, dominated by their castles, for two centuries after the other parts of Spain had been wrested from them.

This province is the home of the smuggler, the gay *contrabandista*, who, by the kindly aid of the English at Gibraltar, brings, duty free, all that women, priests and peasants fancy—a gay, joyous, reckless, well-dressed fellow is he, whom everybody likes. The scenery here is as wild and grand as in any part of Switzerland. The diligence roads are few and the journey must generally be made over wild paths on horseback. The peasants of Spain are generally a strong, able-bodied, independent, polite race of men. They are industrious in their way. The climate makes it necessary to take life easily. The men of the better classes have an intelligent countenance, but a thin, feeble body, as if their powers had been sapped by some dissipation. The men, high and low, everywhere, and at all times, in the railroad car, at the dinner table, between the courses, smoke—forever smoke—never the pipe, not often cigars, but generally the cigarette. Every man has his pouch for tobacco and his paper for making cigarettes, and almost every man will have his thumb and forefinger discolored by the holding of the burning tobacco. The peasant women are small and stout, with coarse, sunburnt features.

The ladies are short, well-formed, inclined to stoutness, with black hair, large dark eyes, long eyelashes, fair complexion, square faces, with features not particularly handsome. There is no variety of feature or of form among them. They all look alike. The hair is always neatly dressed with a braid or roll on the top of the head, and with natural flowers. The ladies as a rule, never wear bonnets. The beautiful mantilla is always worn in the street. It is a black lace vail, sometimes large and sometimes small, which, thrown over the head, falls gracefully upon the shoulders and nearly to the feet, or may be, more closely gathered on the breast and fastened by some pretty ornament. Those who cannot afford this mantilla will wear a silk handkerchief, beautifully colored, tied over the head. The more common people wear a coarser one tied over the head in a similar way.

The charm of the women is not so much in the beauty of the face as in symmetry of form, graceful walk and bearing, and in their style of dress. The lady, and even the little girl, will always have her fan. This seems to be her talisman. She talks with it, flirts with it, fans and hides her face with it, and by its peculiar motions every one knows what its fair possessor thinks and feels.

The standard dress of the gentleman is the capa or cloak, generally of black cloth, with some brilliant lining, with one side thrown over his left shoulder, revealing the brilliant lining as it falls behind. The poor man has his cloak also to cover his rags. This national costume was said to have been adopted for greater facility in carrying and in using concealed weapons, and the attempt to abolish by law the wearing of this garment and the slouched hat which concealed the face, led to a revolution in Madrid some 200 years ago. The custom was stronger than the king, and the people still retain the capa. What law could not do, however, fashion is doing. The young swells and aristocracy of the great cities now are leaving the old Spanish dress for the more fashionable garments of Paris.

PROMINENT POINTS.

A glance at a few prominent points in the history of Spain will make more intelligible what we shall have to say hereafter.

The Phœnicians had colonies in the Southern part, before the foundation of Rome. Andalusia was called by them Tartessus, from whence they derived precious metals, corn and oil. This Tartessus was the destination of Jonah, which he probably would have reached had he not been detained by an unexpected event which removed him to another sphere of usefulness. The Annalists of Spain say that it was first settled by Tubal.

The Greeks also traded with the ports of this country, which was then called Iberia, and many of the cities claim to have been founded by Hercules, as the frequent towns, temples and statues dedicated to him attest. From antiquity his name has been written on the pillars of the Straits between the Atlantic and the Mediterranean.

The Phœnicians seemed to have transferred their allegiance in time to the Carthaginians, and afterward, when the colossal empire of Rome was overshadowing the world, all these colonies submitted to her after a series of bloody wars. It was the battle-ground of Hamilcar, Hannibal and Scipio before the Christian era. The whole country was brought into entire subjection to the Romans about the time of Augustus Cæsar, and called Hispania.

The Romans made the peninsula one of their most prosperous colonies; they introduced all their civilization, laws and customs; built cities, roads, castles and bridges, some of which remain to this day. They educated the whole nation in the arts, agriculture and architecture, and for four centuries under their sway the Spaniards remained a cultivated and civilized people. Seneca and Lucan and the Emperors Trajan, Adrian and Theodosius were born here.

When the Roman Empire began to dissolve from its own corruption, the Visigoths overran and conquered Spain, but brought with them their barbarism. They despised labor and trade, and this quality has ever since adhered to the Spaniard. They intermarried with the original inhabitants and founded a splendid empire, embracing parts of France, all of Spain, and part of Africa, near the Straits.

They adopted the Latin language and the Catholic faith, and from that time the power of the priest has been predominant in Spain. The Goths elected their monarchs in an assembly called the Cortes, consisting of the nobility and the bishops. They took oath to obey him as long as he ruled justly, and *no longer*, but declared the people were greater than the king, and he was their servant. This institution of old Gothic freedom, called the Cortes, of which the English Parliament and States General of France are other examples, although shorn of much of its power, has survived, and has been the bulwark of Spanish liberty, till now it has again re-asserted its ancient prerogatives, and secured again for Spain the form of a good government.

The Goths came into Spain about 409 A.D., and continued in power until 711, when their authority was entirely subverted by the Moors.

Three centuries of indulgence and luxury in the genial climate of Spain had changed the character of these simple and hardy warriors. Intestine divisions had also weakened them, while the authority of Mohammed, then in the first century of its existence, was fired with all the ardor and self-denial of fanaticism.

The head of the Moslem power, at this time, was the Caliph of Damascus. His fiery hordes, carrying their religion with the sword, had extended themselves from Arabia, over Egypt, along the northern coast of Africa, even to the Straits, and they were now attacking the Gothic settlements at Teutan, near the African Pillar of Hercules.

Looking across the Straits to the continent of

Europe, their eyes rested on the charming valleys and fields of Spain. It was a land rich in gold and silver, abounding in mountains, valleys, springs and fruits of every kind, a perfect contrast to the arid plains, and they longed to possess it.

Musa-ben-Nozier, an Arabian, was the commander of the Saracen Army, encamped in Barbary. Roderick, the last of the Goths, was ruler in Spain. One of the most desperate leaders of the Saracens was a tall, lean, sun-burnt warrior from Damascus called Taric el Tuerto, or one-eyed Taric. He sought to lead the daring expedition. With a small army he crossed the Straits, and fortified himself on the rock, now called after him Gibraltar, or, as it was then called, Gebal al Taric, the rock of Taric. He burned his ships behind him, as did Cortez, in Mexico. His followers asked: "How shall we escape, if we do not conquer?" The fiery Saracen answered: "There is no escape for the coward. We must conquer, or die."

"But how shall we return home if we conquer?"

"Your home," replied Taric, "is before you; you must win it with the sword."

In a few days the whole power of Spain was upon his little army. A terrible battle was fought at Xeres, between Seville and Cadiz, and not far from Gibraltar. It raged for three days. The luxurious Goths could not withstand the desperate valor of the Moor; and at last Roderick was slain and the Goths defeated.

Luxury and dissension had weakened the Goths and given them a prey to the Moslem, and the same agents, dissension and luxury, seven centuries later, destroyed forever the Mohammedan power in Spain.

As has so often been the case in the great wars of the world, it is said that there was a woman at the bottom of this great invasion; and the very romantic story is told of how Roderick, the king, became enamored of the beauty of the daughter of Count Julian as he saw her at the bath, and how he violated even kingly authority to possess her, and how in revenge Count Julian invited the Moors to invade Spain, and betrayed his own country into their hands. This romance of Roderick, Count Julian, and his daughter would fill a volume.

To the honor of the Moors, be it said, they brought with them a superior civilization. After the battle of Xeres they spread over the whole country, but they allowed the people to exercise their religion and retain their property on condition of paying tribute.

For about forty years the Moors of Spain acknowledged the authority of the Caliph of Damascus, and he appointed their rulers. But in 758 they declared themselves independent of the Caliphate of

Damascus, and appointed their own Caliph, whose seat was at Cordova. They were a wonderful people, far in advance of their Christian neighbors. The people were industrious, and agriculture flourished. They had plantations of sugar, rice and cotton.

Their cities were filled with merchants, and their ships traded with all parts of the world. They had manufactories of paper, steel, carpets, silk, leather, and gold and silver embroidery. They had schools where chemistry, mathematics, astronomy, philosophy and medicine were taught, and were the first to teach the use of figures and algebraic signs. They had great taste in architecture and in the adornment of their houses and gardens, as the Mosque of Cordova and the Palace of Alhambra and the Moorish cities of Cordova, Seville and Malaga show at the present time.

They essayed to carry the Crescent into France and overrun all Christendom, but received a check at the great battle near Poictiers, fought by Charles Martel, in 732.

They now founded a magnificent kingdom in Spain, which lasted for nearly eight centuries.

There was, however, a portion of the Goths, who inhabited the northern parts of Spain—brave, hardy and independent, living among the Pyrenees and along the Bay of Biscay—who were never conquered by the Moors. These mountaineers sustained their religion and independence, and little by little, century after century, they increased in power, made constant inroads on the land of the Moors, and one by one regained the great cities of Spain from the Moorish yoke.

The great idea of the Christian world, from the 9th to the 12th centuries, was to exterminate the infidel. From this sentiment originated the Crusades to the Holy Land, and in Spain all the power of the Church and of chivalry was centred in this one object. The expulsion of the Moor was a holy crusade. Knights and warriors of all countries flocked to Spain, and vied with each other in daring deeds of valor in fighting the Saracens.

In these times rose the immortal Cid, the greatest hero of Spanish Romance. He took Valencia from the Moors in 1094; St. Ferdinand took Cordova in 1235, and Sevile in 1242. So that at last, in the 13th century, the Moors were driven back to the southern parts of Spain, into the mountains of Grenada and Ronda, which they held until 1492, when the conquest of Grenada was completed and Boabdil, the last Moorish king, delivered the keys of the Alhambra to Ferdinand and Isabella on the 20th of January of that year, and the power of the Moslem, which had existed for nearly eight centuries in Spain, came to an end.

The Christians had gunpowder and cannon—then recently come into use—as their great weapon, with the chivalry and Christianity of Europe leagued with them. The Moslems were, notwithstanding, their equals in valor and in skill, but there were dissensions among them, and this was their ruin.

No tale of romance can be more exciting than the siege of Grenada, as told by Washington Irving, and to read it while traveling through the mountain passes, or in sight of lofty castles, or within the courts of the Alhambra, in full view of the scenes where those daring deeds were performed, is most thrilling.

The century from 1490 to 1590 was one of immense importance to Spain.

It was here at Grenada, during the siege, that Columbus was commissioned by Ferdinand and Isabella to cross the Western Ocean in search of a new passage to the Indies, and which resulted in overwhelming Spain with gold, luxury, power and indolence.

It was in this century that the Inquisition was established, with all its horrors, in Spain, which dwarfed the intellect of the nation for ages.

In this century that the Jews and the Moors, the most industrious classes in Spain, were expelled, and trade and agriculture left to languish for centuries, and even till now. It was in this age, and in Spain, that Ignatius Loyala was born, and Jesuitism, that curse of all Catholic countries, had its rise. All these great events have been fearful curses to Spain. They together swept over her like the besom of destruction, not only prostrating agriculture, trade and commerce, but changing and stultifying the very character of the people.

To one who desires to trace the causes of all these evils, I think it will be found that they at last centre back in their system of religion. The Romish church is answerable for all the consequences of the expulsion of the Jews, the Inquisition and Jesuitism. The history of Spain, from the time of Ferdinand and Isabella, is the record of a sad decline from the highest position among the European powers to the lowest. The more recent troubles in Spain have arisen out of Salic law, or the law which prohibits a female from sitting on the throne. This law, which always prevailed in France, never prevailed in Spain until the time of Philip V, in 1750, when he ordained it as the law of Spain, and it so remained until about 1832, when Ferdinand VII, about to die without a son, repealed the Salic law, so that his infant daughter, Isabella, might become Queen.

On the death of Ferdinand VII, in 1833, Don Carlos, his brother, was the male heir, who would be entitled to the throne in case the Salic law were in force. Of course he claimed that Ferdinand VII, could not repeal the law—but why could he not repeal it if Philip V could ordain it?

But as the throne was the game, each party, as is usual, had convincing arguments, and hence the war of the Carlists in 1833. Don Carlos was defeated and Isabella reigned until 1868, when she was expelled and a republic established.

She then, while in banishment, abdicated in favor of her son, Alfonso XII, the present king.

The recent war by the Carlists has been carried on, on the assumption that the Salic law is still in force, and that Don Carlos is the rightful heir.

MARSEILLES TO BARCELONA.

From France we can enter Spain by one of three ways—from Bayonne by rail to Irun, from Perpignan by diligence over the Pyrenees, or from Marseilles by steamer to Barcelona. We will enter Spain by the last route, and leave it by the first. The steamers from Marseilles to Barcelona make the voyage in twenty-four hours.

The sail from the harbor of Marseilles presents a beautiful picture. The mole which protects the shipping from the swell of the outer harbor is a grand artificial work, and the granite walls, with storehouses erected on them, extend for miles before the city. The Port is filled with the shipping of all countries.

Passing out of the grand entrance to the outer harbor, the city begins to loom up before us, stretching away on to the hills, while far above the harbor, the masts and the churches, on the loftiest eminence, one thousand feet above the city, stands the Church of Notre Dame de la Garde, its tower surmounted by a colossal statue of the holy mother stretching her arms in blessing over the city of which she is the patron saint. She is the last object the sailor sees as the shores recede beyond the waters of the Mediterranean, and the first to greet his view as he makes for the port. We also turn our eyes to her—not in worship, but in admiration—as we steam out of the harbor past the island If, and of Monte Cristo, forever made famous by Dumas.

In twenty hours we are approaching the port of

BARCELONA,

in Catalonia, which constitutes the northwestern portion of Spain. Catalonia has a sea line of about 250 miles, and is the most commercial, industrious, prosperous and rich of all the provinces of the peninsula. It has eight cathedral towns, of which Barcelona and Tarragona are the largest. The Catalans—the Yankees of Spain—are very industrious. The land is well cultivated, and here is the only part of Spain where we have seen the hills terraced and planted with the vine and the olive. You will see the laborers at work before sunrise in the fields. Manufactories of all kinds abound, especially of cotton, and to such an extent that I was informed that Barcelona was the third port for importing cotton in the world, Liverpool and Havre, only, importing more.

Barcelona is surrounded by manufactories of paper, cotton and silk, with tall chimneys, which, rising from among green olive groves, do not present the forbidding appearance of a manufacturing town. The Catalans are quite distinguished from other Spaniards in language, dress and habits. The proud and haughty Castilian cannot understand the patois of the Catalan, and will not recognize these bankers, merchants and manufacturers as gentlemen.

Like all commercial people, they are fond of their liberties, and have always been ready to revolt against their Government and set up a republic. They have been the leaders in nearly every modern insurrection, and have been almost as cruel and bloodthirsty at such times as the French.

All the common people wear the blood-red cap, which is a bag of woolen cloth about a foot long. One end is fitted to the head, and the other is gathered and falls behind or at the side. They have short jackets and long pantaloons. The women wear the mantilla, or a handkerchief of colored silk over the head, and a tight bodice. They have large, black, rather fierce-looking eyes, and one can well suppose that they have a tincture of Arab or Creole blood in their veins. They have more of the characteristics of the French and the Genoese than of the real Spaniard.

Catalonia exports large quantities of wine and oil. In some of the districts it is said that in time of vintage the mud of the streets is blood-red with the refuse of the grape after the juice is pressed out, and that the legs of the peasants, which are the real wine press, are of a rich crimson dye.

To see the dirty, slovenly way of making the wine does not tend to increase one's appetite for the delicious beverage. The wines here are generally thick and black as ink, and called black-strap. They are exported largely to Bordeaux, to enrich poor clarets prepared for the American and English markets.

Another branch of trade in Catalonia greatly interested me, and I took some pains to gather some particulars of it from the people. I refer to the culture and the

MANUFACTURE OF CORK.

The cork is an oak which grows best in poorest soil. It will not endure frost, and must have sea air, and also an altitude above the sea level. It is only found along all the coast of Spain, the northern coast of Africa and the northern shores of the Mediterranean. There are two barks to the tree, the outer one being stripped for use. The cork is valuable according as it is soft and *velvety*. The method of cultivating it is interesting. When the sapling is about ten years old it is stripped of its outer bark for about two feet from the ground; the tree will then be about five inches in diameter, and say six feet up to the branches. This stripping is worthless. The inner bark appears blood-red, and is called the *shirt* of the tree, and if it is split or injured the tree dies. After eight or ten years the outer bark has again grown in, and then the tree is again stripped four feet from the roots. This stripping is very coarse, and is used as floats for fishing nets. Every ten years thereafter it is stripped, and each year two feet higher up, until the tree is forty or fifty years old, when it is in its prime, and may then be stripped every ten years, from the ground to the branches, and will last two hundred years. The third crop is very poor cork, and is used to make the coarsest kinds of stoppers for jars, soles of shoes, etc. It is about twenty years before anything can be realized from the tree, and for this reason the Spaniards, who are not fond of looking after posterity, plant few new trees.

The best cork grows in Catalonia, and is used for

bottling champagne. For this purpose it must be thick, supple, velvety, and free from holes. The generous wines from Xeres (or Sherry) and of Oporto require also a perfect cork.

It is said that over thirty millions of bottles of champagne are manufactured every year, and that the price of champagne corks is from four to eight cents each; and when we consider the immense amount of cork used for other wines, soda, beer, and mineral waters manufactured in England, America and Germany, we shall see that the trade is something enormous. The price of cork has doubled in the last fifteen years, and the owners of cork forests and the speculators in the leases of them have amassed immense fortunes. England furnishes the best market for cork. The cork wood is much used in Russia for the lining of railway carriages and for partitions in houses.

Corks are manufactured largely in the villages of Catalonia, and entirely by hand. Men, women and boys are employed in cutting, assorting, washing and packing them. The men earn from three to four francs, and the women from one and a half to two francs per day. A good workman will cut 1,500 per day, and a woman 1,000. All corks are here cut by hand, from the smallest vial cork up to the bung, by a sharp knife ten inches long and three and a half inches wide. The machine-cut corks of the United

States have a rough, fuzzy coat, and are apt to be imperfect, while the workman by hand only cuts the perfect wood. Corks for the fine wines must be perfect, and only the skilled workman can detect the holes in the centre by the weight.

All Spaniards are averse to novelties, and even the enterprising Catalan will have no labor-saving machines. They still, as all over Spain, plow with a crooked stick, the same thing exactly, as appears from Egyptian monuments, that was used three thousand years ago. They threaten to lynch any one who will introduce a cork-cutting machine. All the houses are built with reference to keeping out heat and draughts. In all country houses no doors open directly from without, but turns are made in the front hall to keep out the air. The houses here, as in all Spain, have no fire-places. My informant, who was an intelligent cork manufacturer and an educated German, says the Catalans are a joyous, happy people, living on little and satisfied; that there are no class distinctions; that poor and rich mingle more together than in any other country; that the women are children of Nature, fond of dress, flowers and amusements; that the daughters of the lawyers and doctors and of the best citizens of the country towns will cut corks to make for themselves spending money; and even the factory girl, who makes twenty cents per day, will spend four cents for flowers; that she will always have fresh flowers in her hair and others in a glass before her when at work; that they have very little education, but great natural gifts of conversation; that the men never, except on great occasions, go to church, but the women go in the morning, and immediately after they go to the rural dance; that they live out-of-doors, often eat out-of-doors; surrounded by a picturesque country, they are fond of scenery and lovers of Nature.

BARCELONA.

ALL Spanish cities are old, and Barcelona is one of the most ancient. The local historian is fond of claiming that Hercules founded this city 400 years before Romulus was born. Be that as it may, it bears the name of Hamilcar Barca, the father of Hannibal, and has ever been a famous port. It is probably the richest and most enterprising of all the Spanish cities. Like Venice and Genoa, it was a higher honor in Barcelona to be a great merchant than to wear the armorial distinctions of a warrior knight. While the old Andalusian and Castilian knights were seeking renown on the tented field the merchant of Barcelona was amassing money by trade in foreign parts. The consequence is, the Barcelonese are rich and cosmopolitan and the Castilians poor and proud.

Barcelona is the best seaport on the eastern coast of Spain. Its natural advantages are considerable as a harbor, but they require an extensive wall to protect them from the easterly winds of the Mediterranean. The first object which attracts the eye, on approaching the city, is the fortress, called Fort Montjuick, which frowns down upon the city from a height of 800 feet. It was probably intended as much to keep the turbulent citizens in check as for a defence for the harbor and town. The view from this fort is very grand. The Mediterranean is before you. Its coast, dotted with villages, can be traced far north to the Pyrenees. The city lies at your feet, while all around in the suburbs, among the green trees, can be seen the tall chimneys of different manufactories.

The city is, for a Spanish city, cleanly and well built, and consists of the old and new parts. The modern city is handsomely built up with large, fine houses divided into flats, which are as elegant as the residences of Paris. A great feature in the outdoor life of a Spaniard is his promenade. Here they spend their evenings and take their exercise. Here the mothers come with their daughters, without bonnets, but with the mantilla thrown gracefully over the head. If the mother is not with the young lady, a very attenuated old duenna attends her in her evening walks, and in Barcelona it is proper thus to parade the streets in fine weather till 12 o'clock at night.

Barcelona has one grand promenade, called the Rambla, extending from the harbor through the city. It is continued into the new part of the town, where it is called the Paseo de Gracia, which consists of five avenues of trees, and is the grand drive of the wealthy people.

The shops of the city are very fine, especially in the display of jewelry, fine dresses and articles of luxury. They are brilliantly lighted in the evening, and there the ladies of the city may be seen shopping or admiring the show till late at night.

Generally the great feature of a Spanish city is its cathedral, and our first visit is ordinarily to it. We first ascend its tower, and obtain a general idea of the size, locality, surroundings, and appearance of the city as a whole. The cathedral of Barcelona is a grand old edifice. It was built on the site of a pagan temple, converted into a mosque by the Moors, and afterward added to and rebuilt into its present form. The roof is very lofty and supported by light, graceful pillars. The high altar is surrounded by a semi-circle of columns, and below it is the crypt where lies the body of Eulalia, the patroness of the city, who was killed by Dacian in 304, A.D. Her body was miraculously revealed to the bishop, in 878, by its sweet smell, and was borne to this, its last resting place, by two kings, three queens, four princesses, and cardinals and bishops without number.

I find in Spain that this *odor of sanctity*, this sweet smell issuing from the body of some saint hundreds of years after his or her death, has been a favorite way of revealing the mortal remains, when the relics or body of a saint were needed to give notoriety to some chapel, church or city. Sometimes, instead of an odor, a bright light reveals to some pious bishop the last resting-place of the holy one, but the sweet smell seems to be the most favorite test. Thus it comes to pass that almost every church and cathedral in Spain has these invaluable relics of departed sanctity, which constitute a centre for the devotion of the people, and often a notoriety which gathers thousands of pilgrims annually from all parts of the kingdom. Barcelona is too practical a city for much of this extreme devotion. The worldly religion of this city of merchants and bankers manifests itself in the various schools and colleges for the teaching of law, medicine and science; in the building of hospitals, while their splendid cathedral remains unfinished and no one frequents it but a few old men and women and beggars. While bishops, priests and choir, to the number of sixty, are performing their grand services with not so many worshipers present, the worldly-minded merchants are devoting their charities and time to these institutions to educate the people and to alleviate suffering.

We were speaking of the cathedral. Even the front, a fine, lofty design, remains unfinished, although all the marriage fees for three centuries have been reserved for this purpose. The front is composed of stucco and paint, and probably will so remain for ages as an argument for pious contributions. There are two singular features about this cathedral which we have not seen out of Catalonia, viz., the numerous belfry towers made of ornamental iron frames, and the multitude of Saracens' heads used as corbels. The head of the Saracen, grim, horrid with pain, or grinning with torture, is used as the water-spout from the roof. It shows how a national sentiment of a people—in this case, hatred of the Moor—stamped itself upon the architecture of the nation and originated one of its peculiar features.

Everywhere in Spain the people are demoralized by the sale of government lottery tickets. These are sold at all prices, from 10 cents upward. Every porter, every waiter at the cafés, boys and women in the street, are selling the tickets for a small commission given by the government. Almost all the poor people are gamblers in lottery tickets. We were at Barcelona about Christmas time, when the drawing takes place. The excitement was extreme among the common people. One old man told me he had bought tickets all his life and spent all he earned in this way, and had drawn one prize.

Christmas and New Year's day are festivals devoted to pleasure, eating and dancing. In preparation for it you will find the streets filled with flocks of live turkeys, and peasants from all parts of the province, with their picturesque dresses, selling them. A particular wafer called neulas and a cake called turrones—made of honey, almonds and sugar, which is the very quintessence of all sweets—are then sold everywhere.

Hotel life is much the same in Spain as in France, but of a lower order. You have chocolate and a roll in your room early in the morning; breakfast of courses, which is really a dinner, at 11 o'clock, and *table d'hôte* dinner at 6. But the smells of the hotels are simply horrible; even in the large cities and in the smaller hotels of the towns they are pestilential. This arises from the want of drainage. Generally there is no water in the house and no connection with any sewer, and the whole house is pervaded with these dreadful odors, such as no people but the Spaniards can produce or endure. The wonder is that the people do not all die of typhoid fever.

Barcelona has now about 170,000 inhabitants, and is a delightful city for a winter residence. The climate is mild, tempered by the breezes from the Mediterranean; the sun, in winter, is warm and genial; storms are rare. Rents, in fine new residences, are cheap, and living at the hotels about two dollars and a half a day. It has great social advantages, being the capital of the Province, the see of a bishop, and the residence of a captain-general, so that visitors do not want for church or military displays. Their university, their commercial, civil, military and art academies have given a social culture to the people, and their constant intercourse with other nations has given them a cosmopolitan character not ordinarily met with in Spain. They have here one of the finest opera-houses in the world, those of Naples and Milan only being superior to it.

It was here in Barcelona that Columbus was received by Ferdinand and Isabella, in April, 1493, after his return from the discovery oft he New World; and here, at the Church El Belim, is deposited the sword of Ignatius Loyola, which he consecrated to the Virgin, before her altar in Monserrat, in 1522.

MONSERRAT.

MONSERRAT is one of the many, and perhaps the most celebrated of the sacred shrines of Spain. It lies about twenty miles northwest of Barcelona, near the Barcelona and Saragossa Railway. Leaving Barcelona before sunrise, we found the peasants working in the fields, and always wearing a red cap, with a long, slouched top. The common people work early and late, but take their siesta from eleven till two o'clock, or later. The heat of midday forbids work, and this circumstance has fixed the almost universal custom of the country in regard to labor. The railroad passes over a country made up of high, bold hills, sloping to the top, and furrowed and broken by gulches worn by water-courses in rainy weather, with higher ranges of mountains in the distance running in every direction. These mountains are often separated by rapid streams, winding their way among them from the higher mountains in the interior to the sea. Along these streams the railroad finds its way, often along high cliffs and through tunnels piercing the red rocks. Hills, mountains and valleys are covered with the vine. Not an inch of land is wasted. Even to the tops of the highest hills, and along the precipitous base of mountains, where a vine will grow, there you will find a terrace well cultivated and tanks for artificial irrigation. Often the mountain sides are blasted out and a place walled up for a vine-covered terrace.

Monserrat is a lofty, jagged mass of rock, about twenty-five miles in circumference, rising up from the ordinary level of the country about four thousand feet. The beautiful river Llobregat winds around its base, furnishing water power for numerous silk and cotton mills.

The name—Monserrat—signifies the saw-like character of the mountain peaks. The range is cleft in sunder by one awful chasm from east to west, and rising four thousand feet high along this chasm are numerous sharp peaks, serrated, smooth, resembling the teeth of a saw in the distance; but on nearer approach they tower above you straight into the clouds, some resembling the teeth of a tiger, some the tusks of elephants, some a sugar-loaf. One, called the head of San Antonio, is much like the head and face of a man. One, an immense lofty rock, is like a sphinx, beside which the Sphinx of Egypt appears like a baby.

Before ascending the mountain we should give a short account of its history, to show how it has gained its sacred character. On one of its rocky heights once dwelt a Norman lord, whom the Moors in the eighth century were not able to expel. To a certain cave on this mountain the people brought a famous image of the Virgin Mary, to prevent its falling into the hands of the Moors. This image was made by St. Luke, in Jerusalem, A. D. 50, and brought by St. Peter to Spain. For centuries the image remained in this cave, forgotten by man. After the expulsion of the Moors, the Virgin, weary of so monotonous a life for her favorite image, revealed its resting-place to some shepherds by a bright light, and afterward to the pious Bishop of Vique by a sweet smell which preceeded from the cave. The Bishop prepared to carry her in great state into Manresa, a town near by, to his cathedral, but after proceeding along the mountain side a little way, the Virgin obstinately refused to go farther; and here afterward, about two thousand feet up the mountain side, in a most sightly and romantic spot, was built her chapel.

In 976 a convent was erected here for the Benedictines, and this became a famous shrine for the Catholic world. Emperors and kings came here and laid their gifts before the Virgin. The monastery became one of the largest and richest in Spain. Philip II opened the splendid chapel, where the Virgin now is, in 1599.

Around this chapel, clinging to the mountain sides, are immense piles of buildings, capable of holding two hundred monks. This monastery was suppressed in 1835, and all but thirteen monks were turned adrift on the cold world. The French plundered this convent in 1810, carried off all the silver ornaments, and defaced and destroyed what was of no use to them, as they did in almost every city of Spain.

We left the railway at Monistrol, about three miles from the foot of the mountain. A diligence conveys us from thence to the monastery, about half-way up the mountain. Looking at the mountain from the north, the top of it looks like the jaw of an immense alligator, with the teeth upward. The sides of the mountain recede upward in terraces, like the Pyramids of Gizeh. Of so much importance is this holy shrine, that the government has constructed and keeps in order a magnificent road, winding up in zigzag course, like the roads of Switzerland, for two thousand feet to the monastery. Here is the chapel and the Virgin, and here we must pass the night in the cold, bare cells of the dead monks, with a stone floor, long ranges of gloomy, empty cells around us, and the vaults of the departed monks beneath us. We have a coarse, clean bed, a jug of water, a towel, and nothing more. A good-natured, frowzy-looking old monk, the only one we saw, conducts us to the oaken door, gives us the long, ancient, rusty key, and, without light or fire in the winter night, we are left to our thoughts. We had been told during the day that one good old monk, long since dead, often wandered among the scenes of his earthly career after nightfall. This added to the interest of the occasion when all was dark and still, and we heard the owls hooting from the shadowy recesses of the old cloisters.

It was a night of weird, strange sensations. Here the great Charles V had come on a pilgrimage; here also, his son Philip II paid his devotions. Here, in the chapel, Loyola, in 1522, after watching all night before the image of the Virgin in prayer and fasting, dedicated himself to her service and laid his sword on her altar, which is now preserved at Barcelona. Here monks and anchorites from all the noble families and royal houses of Spain spent their lives, never departing from these walls, and their bones lie mouldering in the crypts below. But however weird and strange were our thoughts at night in these gloomy, forsaken cloisters, with owls and bats for our companions, the morning dispelled all such gloom. We could see the sunrise on the high peaks over us, while the valleys were all dark below. The mist was rising over the river which threaded its way far below us down through the valleys. The white villages one by one came out through the mists as the sun rolled them up the mountain sides.

Those old monks had chosen a glorious place for their home. The chief object of interest at the monastery now is the chapel of the Virgin, containing her image, her dresses, and the room full of votive offerings which have been made to her. The chapel is a large, fine church, but its best things have been carried away by the French. We cannot but admire the boldness of the undertaking to build so massive a church on this inaccessible height. The Virgin is raised to a little gallery over the high altar. She is dressed up in tawdry finery, ribbons and tinselry. She is made of black wood, and holds a child on her lap and a ball in her right hand. One room behind the high altar is devoted to the safe-keeping of the votive offerings made to the Virgin in return for miracles wrought. The room is filled with a great medley of articles, among which are faces, legs, arms, hands and feet, cut from marble; crutches, canes, military hats and coats worn in battles, with the former owners' names attached; rude pictures, representing great deliverances, most of them coarse and ridiculous, as if intended for caricatures. For example, one represents a man with a donkey-cart struck by a railroad train. The donkey and cart are thrown into the air, the donkey with his feet upwards and the cart on the top of the man, and all tumbling in mid-air over a precipice. Another, a little chap falling down stairs and yelling most lustily; another, a child falling out of a window; people on sick beds praying to the Virgin. These are fair specimens of hundreds of pictures which, framed and hung around the room, attest the wonder-working power of the Virgin. All this trumpery shows what a hold the worship of Mary has on the people, high and low; but the most significant fact showing this is that sixty thousand persons annually come on pilgrimage to the monastery of Monserrat to pray before this Virgin.

While we were there, one poor creature, an old woman, arrived on foot from Naples, and peasant women from the country, with some burden on their hearts, had come to get relief from the holy mother.

When our party were admitted to the gallery where the Virgin was, these poor creatures pressed in, and it was a sight which brought tears to the eyes to see them weeping, clasp the Virgin's feet and tell her their sorrows and supplicate her help.

As yet we are only half way up Monserrat. From the monastery to the highest point of St. Jeronimus it is two thousand feet. The path lies along the face of a fearful chasm, which divides the mountain from east to west. It is said, that it was rent in twain on the day of the crucifixion. From the monastery to the top of St. Jeronimus, scattered along the steep and difficult path, are twelve stations or hermitages, each perched on some lofty and almost inaccessible rock. The one, on the top of the highest point, is called the Hermitage of St.

Jeronimus; another, St. Andrus; another, Santiago, until nearly the whole calendar of the saints is emblazoned upon these weather-beaten points. The way up along the chasm which divides the mountain runs along high, dizzy cliffs, ascends by steps cut in the rock, passing these hermitages one after the other. It is called the *Via Crucis*. All these hermitages were once filled with anchorites, who lived each in his cell alone on these lofty heights, from which he never departed alive after he had once entered it; and yet, it is said, these cells were eagerly sought as a great prize by the devotees of those days. The view from the top of St. Jeronimus is exceedingly grand. We stood there as the sun went down; the blue sea was far to the east; the whole country, seen from the top, was broken into undulating hills, rising into mountains; the Pyrenees rose far away on the northern horizon, covered with snow; mountains abounded everywhere; and from these lofty pinnacles, looking below, it appeared as if a tumultuous sea had been suddenly petrified in its most angry commotion; the beautiful Llobregat wound like a thread of silver at our feet, and a few miles away in the valley, just before us, at the north, lay the city of Manresa; and near by it the cave where Loyola passed a whole year in penance before he devoted himself to the Virgin at Monserrat, and where, it is said, he wrote his book—the rules of his famous order—under the very eyes of the Virgin, who looked from her lofty and jagged throne, on Monserrat, with smiles, down upon her faithful knight keeping vigils in his lonely cave.

BARCELONA TO MADRID.

OUR route will now lead us from Barcelona nearly due west, out of Catalonia into Arragon, to the old city of Saragossa. The whole journey is through a picturesque country, clothed with vines and abounding in cork and olive trees. We wind through beautiful valleys, over high cliffs, through frequent tunnels, passing no considerable town until we arrive at Lerida, about 112 miles.

This city has been a post of military importance and the key to Catalonia since the days of the Romans. The armies of Cæsar and Pompey, Saracen and Christian, Wellington and Napoleon, have in turn fought for it.

Here, if the annals are to be believed, died Herodias and her daughter Salome. While performing their dances on the frozen river, the ice broke, and both were drowned; but the head of Salome was cut off by the sharp edge of the ice, and from the very force of early habit the bodiless head continued its dance, and so the Baptist was avenged.

SARAGOSSA.

THIS city, the capital of Arragon, named after Cæsar Augustus, is on the Ebro, and has been famous in all history for its military importance. It was one of the great centres of Roman civilization, and here was born the first Christian poet, Aulus Prudentius, about 348, who has been styled by the critic Bentley the Horace and Virgil of the Christians, and who celebrated in song the edict of the Roman Senate which forbade the worship of idols and established the Christian religion, which dethroned Jupiter and enthroned Christ. The city is divided by the Ebro which is a noble stream, spanned by a splendid stone bridge, first built by the Romans. It boasts of two cathedrals, neither of which is distinguished for antiquity or architecture. The more modern one is called the Cathedral el Pilar, because it contains the identical pillar on which the Virgin descended from heaven. One of its chapels contains an image of the Virgin and Child, in black wood, rude and coarse, but very sacred. It is said that fifty thousand pilgrims have come to this sacred shrine in one year. It is a Bethesda for the lame, halt and blind, who come here to be healed if the Virgin is propitious. It is also a harvest field for beggars, and here they congregate in great numbers. The city from without with its massive walls, pierced by eight gates, its tall towers, spires and cupolas give it a grand appearance. Within, the streets are narrow, dirty and the houses dilapidated. It has one fine thoroughfare called the Coso.

Its churches were plundered by the French, and its fine old castles were riddled by shot and shell during the two famous sieges by the French in 1808, commanded by Marshals Lannes, Junot, Mortier and Moncey, in which were sacrificed needlessly 60,000 brave soldiers. The leaning tower of San Felipe is worthy of comparison with the famous tower of Pisa.

From Saragossa to Madrid, by rail, is a journey of twelve hours, made in the night.

MADRID

is a city built on a high plateau, surrounded by bleak and barren plains, with a treacherous climate, glaring with heat in summer and subject to severe, chilling winds in winter. Puerta del Sol, once the eastern gate, is now the heart of the city, from whence, like arteries, all the large streets radiate. It is a square upon which, or near which, are congregated all the fashionable shops and saloons, and through which flows the life and fashion of the city. The Prado, extending along the eastern side of the city, is beautifully laid out as a park with walks and groves, and is the Central Park of Madrid. It is a modern city first brought to notice by the Emperor Charles V, who regarded its climate a panacea for his bodily ills. His son, Philip II, removed the seat of government to it in 1560 from Valladolid. There is nothing in its position or surroundings to recommend it as the site of a great city. It has no military importance; it guards no pass or fruitful vega, and is surrounded by no agricultural interests. Nothing but the whim of Royalty could have made it a great capital. It imports everything from a long distance, and manufactures nothing.

It has no cathedral or ancient buildings of note, yet there are places of interest which we cannot omit to mention. The Royal Palace is one of the finest in Europe. It is situated on the western side of the city, overlooking the Valley of the Manzanares and a wide sweep of country to the west, reaching to the Guadarrama mountains, which, standing in rugged and lonely grandeur, covered with snows, limit the view in that direction. The palace was intended to surround a square, and to be 470 feet on each side and 100 feet high. It was laid out on a scale so grand that it would have rivaled the Tuileries, but it has never been finished. Only one side of this immense pile is completed. It is a palace 450 feet long, built of white stone resembling marble, and stands nearly 100 feet high. The Spaniards are fond of display, and the palace shows all the magnificent variety of tapestry, velvet, gorgeous furniture, rich marble and mosaics generally found in princely mansions. The stables interested me more than the palace. There were about 150 horses for the use of the young king, embracing his household coach horses, driving-horses and saddle-horses, Each had a name over his stall. They were reared in Spain, France and England. The Spanish horses, especially the Andalusian, did not show the finest points. They had short, heavy bodies; long tails, held close to the body; tapering necks; fine thick breasts, but short, hollow backs. The carriages were superb. I counted one hundred of all sorts and sizes ranged in an immense room.

There were some ten or twelve state coaches used from the time of Ferdinand and Isabella down. They were covered with gold and inlaid with ivory on the outside, and lined with Gobelin tapestry, satin, gold and silver cloth within. One of these was the carriage of Crazy Jane, daughter of Ferdinand and Isabella, and mother of Charles V, who is said to have carried her husband's body in its coffin with her for forty years, until her death. The harness is made in the royal stables, and are the most magnificent trappings that horses ever wore. There is a guard of twenty horse and about one hundred foot soldiers always on duty around the palace, and they are relieved every two hours. All this, for a country which is hopelessly in debt, appears a most extravagant display. These appendages of royalty are finer, perhaps, than those of any crowned head in Europe.

There is a naval museum at Madrid, which has two things which interest an American. One is the exact model of the vessel in which Columbus crossed the Atlantic in 1492, and a chart of the world, on parchment, said to have been made by him on this voyage. This chart resembles very much the photographic pictures of the moon, which we see now a days. His portrait, and those of Cortez and Pizarro, may be seen here.

The Armeria Real is near the palace. It is the finest collection of ancient armor I have ever seen. It is arranged in a hall 227 feet long. Here are gathered the armor and the weapons worn by the great heroes in Spain for centuries past. Along the centre of the room are arranged equestrian figures, completely covered with the identical armor worn by different knights and kings. Along the sides of the rooms are standing figures, also arrayed in their complete panoply of helmet, breast-plate and coat of mail. Here are the helmets worn by Hannibal and Julius Cæsar. There are a number of suits of armor worn by Charles V, most exquisitely wrought. One is the very suit in which he entered Tunis in triumph, and is called Borgonota. The shields are as elaborately wrought as the famous shield of Achilles, and seem to have been patterned from it. Some of the armor is beautifully chased and wrought in black enamel and gold. All are specimens of fine arts after the style of Cellini. Here are the swords of the Cid, of St. Ferdinand, of Ferdinand and Isabella, of Pizarro and Cortez, Don John of Austria, the hero of Lepanto, and of a host of others. Here is the armor of Columbus as Admiral of Spain. The whole armory is full of these relics of great heroes. They are so arranged as to illustrate the improvements in weapons and defence from the earliest to modern times.

This is one of the most interesting objects in Madrid. There is another place which has a mournful interest for Protestants—that is the Plaza Mayor. This is the old grand square of Madrid, where the royal bull-fights were celebrated, and where the Inquisition held the *auto-da-fé*. The square is 400 feet on each side, and in the centre is a fine equestrian statue of Philip III, by John of Bologna. When the trials and the executions of the *auto-da-fé* were held, a great platform was erected for the judges of the Inquisition on one side of the square. The front rooms and balconies fronting on the square were reserved for the royal family, the noblemen and the clergy. The seat of the king was on the balcony in the centre of the north side of the square, where are now seen the royal arms on the front of the house. The populace crowded in and filled the square. Thus, under the countenance of the king, in the presence of all the high dignitaries of the Church, arrayed in their priestly robes, the culprits were brought forth to be tried by the judges of the Inquisition, who were accusers, judge and jury. The trial generally commenced early in the morning and lasted the whole day, and ended in the lurid fires which consumed the wretched victims and gave a grand finishing stroke to the spectacle which was intended to strike terror into the hearts of all beholders. This accursed institution did its work well, and accomplished what was intended by it. Ferdinand first established it in Seville in 1481. He was a grasping, crafty prince. His object was to extort money, terrify his opponents, and revenge himself on his enemies. The Church used it as an engine to extirpate heresy and to perpetuate its power. Working in secret, its mysterious agents scattered everywhere, invincible in power, from whom no secrets were hid, omniscient and omnipresent, it struck a dread fear to the heart of every Spaniard, and locked his soul in suspicion against every man; froze all the sweet and tender sympathies of social life; destroyed confidence and trust in his fellows, and shut the door on hospitality. Three centuries of this discipline has made the haughty, reserved, suspicious Spaniard what he is to-day. The sweet amenities of social life are not known among them. Every man lives in and for himself. Every man suspects his neighbor. Revenge is a national trait, and the dagger of the assassin has ever been the familiar weapon to execute his behest. In days gone by no Spaniard was without this weapon concealed under his cloak, and the city of Madrid was nightly the scene of some secret murder.

The effect sought by the Church to be produced

by the Inquisition has been accomplished. Men dared not think for themselves. The yoke of priestcraft was fastened on them; they became, body and soul, the property of the Church, and subject to her dictation, till they can no longer think or reason for themselves. The Inquisition, or the Holy Tribunal, as they called themselves, since its organization in Spain alone, burned 3,460 persons alive, 18,000 in effigy, imprisoned 288,000 from 1481 to 1808, and they confiscated the goods of all these persons to the use of the king or the Church. It expelled the Moors and the Jews, who were their most industrious and commercial people; it destroyed all enterprise and progress in the development of their resources; and thus Spain became a nation of grandees, priests and peasants, without education, without industry, and without commerce.

The crime has been great. Its lurid fires have lighted up ages of persecution. But Nemesis is now demanding and taking her satisfaction.

THE MUSEO.

The most attractive object to the stranger in Madrid is the Museo, or the gallery of paintings. It is far from being as large as some other galleries in Europe, and yet I think there is no other which, in interest, excels it. It has pictures by most of the great masters, with this advantage, that nearly every picture is a gem; and it has what no other gallery has—the pictures of Velazquez and Murillo in all their glory. A respectable Velazquez can be found nowhere else; neither can Murillo, in all his richness and beauty as a Conception painter,—as he is called in Spain, or as a painter of saints,—be seen out of this kingdom. He is best known in other European galleries by his beggars and peasants, which were not the efforts of his more mature genius. This gallery comprises some of the best pictures of Raphael, Guido, Van Dyke, Claude, Titian, Rubens and Albert Durer.

The extraordinary merit of this collection is accounted for from the fact that Charles V, living at the time when painting was at its zenith, was a great patron of the arts, as were also his successors, and they invited the great masters to the Spanish court and treated them with distinction and intimacy. Titian, Velazquez and Rubens produced some of their best works at Madrid while they were entertained at the royal palace. As these royal personages were lovers of art, and their sway extended at different times over the German Empire, Naples and Netherlands, they gathered from those countries and sent to Spain the best productions of the most distinguished artists. Did this gallery possess nothing more than the sixty-four pictures by Velazquez, forty by Murillo, ten by Raphael, and forty-three by Titian, it would be considered one of the finest in the world. This is the centre of attraction in Madrid, and the traveler will not be satisfied to finish a day of sight-seeing without a daily visit to the Museo, and for the same reason that in Rome one finds himself almost daily wandering into St. Peter's, or in Paris into the Louvre. When all things else fail, these are ever fresh and full of new beauties never seen before.

This gallery was opened in 1819 with only about 300 pictures, which were gathered from the different palaces belonging to the crown. Additions have been made from time to time from the crown collections, until now there are about 3,000 pictures in the collection. We cannot pretend to the high honor of being an art critic, but no one can visit the great galleries of Europe and linger over these inspirations of beauty and loveliness by Raphael, Murillo and Correggio, without some discipline of the eye and taste which will enable him to tell what he likes and why he likes; and no man need be ashamed that his taste, his appreciation for the beautiful, differs from another. We are all made to differ in such matters. We may, therefore, be pardoned for a few thoughts on this gallery, which is so unique and little known.

The most striking pictures here, although I think not the most pleasing, are those by Velazquez.

Spain was his home; here he was appreciated and rewarded by royal honors. There is great originality in his pictures, and perfect naturalness. He has no ideality, no high sense of the beautiful. He always fails in his virgins and saints and sacred subjects from want of ideality—this quality of uniting in one face all that is heavenly, and excluding all that is earthly, as Raphael could do. His women are women and his men are men, just as you see them, with all that is human and earthly about them. He was a painter of men *par excellence;* men of all classes, kings, dwarfs, peasants, soldiers. His strong, manly nature comprehended what he saw and fixed it on the canvas; but women, gods, goddesses, virgins, saints, any subject which required a combination of ideal qualities, was beyond him. He paints Vulcan as a grimy, ordinary blacksmith; the Virgin Mary as a sedate matron; the divine Father as a bald-headed old gentleman. His portraits, especially the equestrian, are exceedingly fine. His horses seem to move toward you out of the canvas. His pictures of common life —dwarfs, peasants and revellers—are inimitable from the perfect naturalness. He introduces dogs and horses which are as fine as Landseer's.

His landscapes are wonderful from their depth, their coolness, produced by a light gray or bluish color. The details are few, but these are such as you can feel in all their natural freshness. You almost see the cool air; you certainly feel it. You are as conscious of the long, deep, shady vistas, as if you were walking under the trees amid the fountains, and along the purling streams. One or two pictures we cannot forbear naming. One, called Æsop, represents the philosopher in the coarse attire of a peasant. But a few touches in the dark, tawny color, shaded only by slight traces of white, reveal the coarse, keen, defiant wit which would have done honor to a Diogenes. One is astonished to see how so little coarse paint can say so much. As a rule, all his pictures which attempt the higher or the tender sentiments are failures; but there is one exception which we must name. It is the Crucifixion. It is a single figure on a plain cross; darkness gathers over the earth; the cold body, of light gray color, has the first pallor of death stealing over the freshness of life; it stands out from the cross; thorns crown the head; the long hair hangs down on one side of the face, covering the ear; the head is drooping, and the blood is trickling down from under the thorns, over the forehead, down the body, and bathing his very feet and the cross; the face is of a calm and heavenly sweetness; no pain, no grief, but you can almost hear the dying lips breathing "It is finished." It is a single figure on a plain cross, yet it speaks the depth of the sentiment of that awful tragedy.

Few artists can treat this subject without offence

to some sentiment of our nature. The truth, nature and manliness of Velazquez are all his own. Titian had preceded him at the Spanish court, and all his great pictures, with all their fine sentiment and gorgeous coloring, were before him. Yet Velazquez is as unlike Titian as an artist well could be. Without ideality, without the power of delineating the tender and the sentimental, he had the rare power of reproducing nature as he found it. He lived in the time of Philip III, and Philip IV, and died 1660.

MURILLO,

the pupil of Velazquez, was born at Seville, 1618, and was only nineteen years younger than his master. He lived, painted and died at Seville, although a few of his good pictures have crossed the Pyrenees, yet he is only to be seen in all his grandeur in his own native land. There is only one fine Conception of his out of Spain, and this was stolen by Marshal Soult, carried to Paris and sold to the Louvre for $200,000, where it now hangs as one of the gems of that renowned gallery; but in Spain there are numerous conceptions by Murillo, all of which much resemble one another. Velazquez painted for kings, and had the selection of his subjects and the freedom of his own treatment. Murillo painted for the Church, and was controlled in his subjects and modes of treatment, and confined to sacred scenes, such as

Conceptions, the Holy Family, and Adoration of Saints. Like Raphael, he reproduces his principal subjects in all his pictures. With differences of color, grouping and other details his faces of the Virgin, of St. Francis, and St. Augustine, are always the same. It is often said that Murillo's Virgins are only good-looking Spanish peasants. They do lack the heavenly purity and the celestial grace and benignity of Raphael's Virgins, but they combine wonderful sweetness and tenderness. They are women, but they are beatified women, with a celestial light shining in their faces. No man, in our opinion, has ever painted a saint equal to Murillo. In one of his pictures the youthful Jesus is standing on an open Bible placed on a table; St. Francis is looking up into his face and extending one arm to clasp him. The combination of humility, love and adoring faith in the longing, yearning, earnest look of the saint, is something heavenly. There is a wealth of grace, beauty and coloring in his Conceptions, with the Virgin standing in the new moon, gorgeous in her blue robes, surrounded by clouds of golden splendor, attended by myriads of beautiful, joyous cherub faces.

It is impossible to particularize the pictures of Murillo in this gallery. They are all charming. There are three different styles to be traced in Murillo's pictures. The Spaniards call them—first, the *frio*, his earlier style, which is of dark coloring, clear outline and good drawing; of this style are his Beggar-boys, at Munich. Second, the *calido*, or warm, where his coloring is lighter and more sunny, and the outline less defined. Third, the *vaporoso*, or misty, where he so mingles his colors as to throw a golden vapor over all his figures through which the outline is dimly seen. He was a master of colors, and, however extravagant they may appear in detail, their combination is charming.

All the originals of Raphael in the Museo are master-pieces. Here is his celebrated Holy Family, called the Pearl. It once belonged to Charles I, of England, was sold by Cromwell, bought by the Minister of Philip IV, for $10,000, which then was an enormous price. A large number of other pictures were bought with it and sent to Spain. When Philip saw this picture he exclaimed, "This is the pearl of my pictures;" and ever since it has been called by Spaniards, *The Perla*. This picture is different from most of Raphael's. It has not the golden sunset coloring usual with him. It is darker, with a crimson tinge of flesh color. But the light and smile on the face of the infant Jesus looking up to that of his mother, is almost an inspiration.

TITIAN.

Of all the galleries in Europe none can boast of a finer collection of Titians. He was the friend of

Charles V, and Philip II, and painted for them here for three years. After his death Velazquez was deputed to purchase from Venice some masterpieces of this great artist. In the Museo are forty-three magnificent pictures by him, some very large. Here is the noted picture called the *Gloria*, by some considered his master-piece. It is a sort of an apotheosis of Charles V, in which the Trinity, the Virgin, Moses and Elijah, Charles V, and his son, Philip II, and numerous saints appear. This picture, the Emperor directed in his will, should be hung before his tomb; and so it was until he was removed to the Pantheon in the Escorial.

Time will fail to tell of all the other great worthies whose works are gathered here. There are sixty-two pictures by Rubens, with all the usual virtues and faults of this prolific artist. Here, as everywhere, he revels in stout women of roseate hue.

We cannot mention the other great foreign artists. Their fame belongs to other countries; but we should not omit a few more who have been an honor to Spain. Joanes is a painter of sacred subjects. One of his best pictures here is a Descent from the Cross, which is very fine. Alonzo Cano is a painter of great merit. His time was mostly devoted to sculpture. His Crucifixions in wood are found in many cathedrals in Spain, and they are always exceedingly pathetic. His wood-carvings of saints are among the finest specimens of this art. There is at the Museo a fine painting of St. John at Patmos and a Dead Christ, which is a favorite subject with him.

Zurbaran was a Spaniard, and is said to have been unequaled as a painter of monks and friars. Ribera, or Spagnoletto, was a distinguished Spanish artist. His best pictures are here. He was contemporary with Velazquez and Murillo. He delineated suffering, fortitude and martyrdom with wonderful vividness and power. No sentiment of tenderness or pathos ever entered his heart. You can see the martyr in his agony, despising suffering and nerving his quivering frame up to a lofty endurance.

KING ALFONSO.

Before leaving Madrid we should like to speak of a few men of note there. The king, Alfonso XII, is a young man, now (1883) only twenty-five years of age. He has a slim, delicate frame, pale face, and is as unlike his mother, the ex-Queen Isabella, as possible. She is a very large, red-faced, and rather coarse-looking woman. He was for a short time educated at the military school in England, but has received most of his training at Vienna. He still employs tutors, and studies three hours a day. He is said to have some capacity for business, and to fulfill his kingly duties much better than King Amadeus did. His parentage on his father's side is considered doubtful, but Queen Isabella insists that this is of no importance—she is his mother. The young king, however, has a glorious future before him, if he is equal to it. If he proves himself the man to rule in these times; able to grapple with the difficulties around him; if he can see the wants of Spain, and will apply himself with all the prestige of his royal name and kingly office to redress them; will labor to elevate and educate Spain; will spurn the priestly yoke and break it from the neck of his people, he will become one of the illustrious monarchs of the age. The people are ready to hail such a king, to obey him, to adore him, if they can have peace and a fixed government. The difficulties which he or any government have to contend with are great. There are five which we can mention, which press upon Spain like an incubus:

1st. The question of dynasty. Is Alfonso the lawful king, or Don Carlos?

2d. The religious question. Shall there be a State religion? Shall there be liberty of worship, education, and of the press, and shall there be no connection between Church and State?

3d. Shall there be a monarchy or a republic?

4th. The financial question. Spain is hopelessly in debt. She cannot pay her interest. She is, and has been, borrowing money for years at a usurious rate to keep the government going, and it is said that it is a great part of the business at Madrid to speculate in the obligations of the government. Her people are taxed to the utmost, and still there is no possibility of paying their interest. They are hopelessly insolvent. They owe one billion and five hundred millions of dollars.

5th. Civil war may break out at any moment between the Government and the Carlists.

Most nations have only one of these great questions to meet; but Spain has them all pressing her at once, and how she is to come out of them no one can foresee. Such men as Gomez, Castelar and Martinez are leaders on some of these questions, and they will not be put down. The government may be reactionary for the present on the subject of religious liberty and slavery, but they can have no peace while these great leaders of public opinion live.

The civil list of the king is fixed at $600,000. It seems impossible to support the royal court, in the style in which he lives, on that sum. The king pays court to the soldiers, parades with them, mixes with the people, and is affable to strangers.

Don Antonio Canovas del Castillo, the recent President of the Council of Ministers, is a lawyer, and has worked his way up from the common people. There was only one Minister in the Cabinet during his Presidency from the nobility. Canovas is an excellent debater, and the defence of government measures in the Congress of Deputies rested upon him. He is a short man, rather stout, with a slight cast in his eye; a very ready speaker, and is regarded as a man of high character, as that term is understood in Madrid. The President of the Council has a salary of six thousand dollars and the use of the elegant mansion of the President.

He gives a reception every Friday evening. No invitations are given, but the foreign Ministers, the members of the government and Deputies of his own party are expected to attend. Through the kindness of the American Minister, I had the pleasure of attending one of these receptions. The house was immense. We entered from a porte-cochère, up a wide staircase, with beautiful shrubs and flowers on each side; and were received by four servants in livery in the ante-room, where our coats were ticketed and our hats given to us to carry in our hands.

The rooms opened were a suite of three, of immense size, on three sides of an open court, in the centre of the house. The rooms were furnished with gilt furniture, covered with red satin, which was ranged around the sides of the room. The carpets were elegant, and the rooms brilliantly lighted with chandeliers of crystal pendants. All the Ministers of the government were present and all the foreign

Ministers. There was most hearty accord between our government and Spain, as was evident from the warm reception given to our Minister. When the President saw Mr. Cushing, the American Minister, he immediately came up to him and embraced him cordially and with great sincerity. The government had great confidence in Mr. Cushing, in his learning, wisdom and fairness. Probably no foreign Minister at the court had the influence which he had. This influence was not confined to the government, but he was held in the highest estimation by the other Ministers. They consulted him upon difficult questions of international law. He was an encyclopedia of knowledge, of prodigious memory, spoke nearly every modern language, and knew the history of Spain better than the Spaniards themselves. I was proud to see the pre-eminent position which he held among the foreign Ministers. As the Spaniards never spend money on entertainments or give State dinners, no refreshments were given except tea, coffee, cakes, wine and a few sweet drinks, flavored with orange, almonds and other fruits. It was a company of well-bred gentlemen, gathered from every civilized nation on the globe.

HOUSE OF DEPUTIES.

Before leaving Madrid we must look into the Congress, where the House of Deputies meet. It is a large, well-furnished room, with seats in circular form, facing the President's chair, and rising one above the other as they recede. The members seemed in the prime of life, a practical, gentlemanly, well-dressed body of men. They spoke with some animation, but happened to be very prosy. On each side of the Speaker stood a sort of sergeant-at-arms, holding an immense mace and dressed most elaborately in uniform covered with gold lace.

Mr. Canovas sits near the Speaker's chair, in a side seat, so that he can see any member who is speaking. The House is divided into about five parties, some leaders having no more than one follower beside themselves, and some having only one with themselves. The most conspicuous man, after Mr. Canovas, is Mr. Castelar. I had imagined him a tall, thin, pale, student-like looking man, of negligent dress and manners. I had the pleasure of calling on him at his house and of seeing him in the Congress. He is a short, thick-set, florid man; a very genial face, but not strong; no marked characteristics about him; a man no one would remark in the streets. As I saw him he was carefully dressed, ready to speak that evening. He speaks with ease, but after most careful preparation; all his fine figures are elaborately wrought out and then as if delivered on the inspiration of the moment. He prepares himself carefully, much as Mr. Everett did.

When he speaks the House is filled, and for hours you will see the common people gathering around the door for admission.

He has always a most beautiful ornate essay or some grand original theory drawn from books or study, but which has never been tried. His impulses are always generous, noble and winning; he has a wealth of illustration drawn from history. He speaks rapidly and firmly, and always carries with him the whole House, friend and foe, and frequently the whole body, without an exception, will rise and cheer him with great excitement.

When the effort is over, the practical debater, Mr. Canovas, begins to pick flaws in the delicately spun theory; to pull out thread by thread; to knock away this leg and then another, and to ask hard questions. Then Mr. Castelar is at fault. He is an orator, but no debater. He has no repartee, no ability to turn the thrust. He gets confused, and perhaps confounded, and when the vote comes, the eloquent speech, which read so well, which the House applauded, has fallen flat, without a supporter. The practical man has destroyed the theorist.

Mr. Castelar is a native of Malaga. After a university education he devoted himself to a professorship of history in Madrid, with very small emoluments, but he wrote for reviews and essays on historical subjects connected with his studies. He is a sincere Republican, and his theory has always been,—and he has written much upon it,—that Spain should be a federal republic, after the model of the United States Government, which would allow each province to administer their own peculiar *fueros*, or ancient laws, and would harmonize the different sections of the country. He had other beautiful theories. But when he came to rule as President of the Republic, no one of his theories would work. Notwithstanding this, he is a man capable of magnetizing the *people*. His theories are in sympathy with liberty and with their rights. He will always be the leader of reform outside of the Cortes, and great principles in the mouth of such a man will make their way among the people. He is a sincere Catholic of the ancient type, seeking to purify the Church. He is a bachelor, and lives in a pleasant part of the city, in a most unpretending way, on the third story of a flat, with his sister. As the Deputies receive no pay, he is dependent on his writings for his subsistence. But having been Premier, although only for a few months, he is entitled to an annuity of $2,500.

ROMANISM AND PROTESTANTISM.

Of all countries in the world, Spain is the most profoundly Catholic. For centuries the King or

Queen has received from the Pope, the title of his or her Catholic Majesty. As the Catholic religion has here had the fullest sway and has here had time to work out its legitimate influence, it would be worth the trouble of the historian and the moralist to trace its effect on this nation. Let us state the facts fairly, and leave the reader to judge whether the national religion has elevated or debased the morals of the people—has been a friend or an enemy to all true progress. Trace its influence in social life on one class only, and that in which, if in any, it ought to show its purifying and ennobling power—I mean the clergy. No religion can elevate any people above the lives and morals of its ministers. Spain has from time immemorial been cursed with a priesthood noted for their profligacy and sensuality. In the time of Queen Isabella, all orders of ecclesiastics are represented as "wallowing in all the excesses of sloth and sensuality;" and so abhorrent was the evil to the pure mind of the Queen that she put forth all the powers of her prerogative and invoked the aid of her great Cardinal Ximenes, and of the Pope also, to abate it. Even the law was obliged to countenance concubinage in the clergy, and the ancient *fueros* of Castile permitted their issue to inherit the estates of such parents as died intestate. The effrontery of these legalized concubines of the clergy at length became so intolerable that laws were repeatedly passed regulating their apparel and prescribing a badge to distinguish them from virtuous women.

Although more respect is outwardly paid to good morals at this day by the ecclesiastics, yet it is notorious that in Spain purity of life is not expected in the clergy. As one gentleman in Spain expressed it to me, every priest is supposed to have his housekeeper, and her position in the establishment is well understood. It is, however, just to say that the lives of the higher dignitaries of the Church are more exemplary than those of the inferior clergy. If such is the character of the priests, it is easy to see how demoralizing to a people is the religion which can palliate or endure them.

I have been asked, "What chance for Protestantism is there in Spain?" A few facts and figures will help to answer this question. Out of 16,500,000 inhabitants in Spain all but 60,000 are Catholics by profession. Of these 60,000, very few can properly be called Protestants. All the power, all the nobility, all the education, all the money, are enlisted on the side of the Church. The women are all devotees under the influence of priests. They, only, attend the services. The men were educated Catholics and must have a religion to die by, as they desire to be buried in the odor of sanctity. Therefore they are Catholics. The serious, educated and thinking men who believe in religion are Catholics of the Döllinger school, and believe in reforming their own Church, but never intend leaving it. Such is Castelar, who is a sincere Catholic, while at the same time he repudiates many of the assumptions and practices of the modern Catholic Church.

Spain has been, and probably is now, the most priest-ridden of all the European kingdoms; yet a slight comparison of figures will show that even Spain is making rapid strides in ridding herself of the priestly yoke. In 1833 there were connected with the Church, including monks and nuns, 175,000 persons, or one to about ninety-five inhabitants. Of these, about 90,000 were prelates and priests connected with the cathedrals and parishes. In 1836 all conventual establishments were suppressed and their property confiscated. This gave rise to long disputes with the Pope, which were at last settled by a concordat in 1859 by which the government was authorized to sell all ecclesiastical property except churches and parsonages, and to give in return an equal amount of government certificates, untransferable, bearing interest at the rate of three per cent. Inasmuch as Spanish stocks are at a low ebb and the Government are unable to pay their interest, it is to be presumed that the Church will not be the gainer by this concordat. But now for the effect. At the present time there are connected with the Church, as prelates and priests, less than 40,000 persons. This leaves but one priest to about 400 inhabitants, including men, women and children. There are forty-three bishops and nine archbishops, the Archbishop of Toledo being the Primate of all Spain. By the Constitution of 1875 the Catholic religion is declared to be the religion of the State. As Protestants in all countries are largely interested in the religious liberty question in Spain, we copy in full the article of the Constitution on which they all rely for liberty of opinion, worship and teaching:

Article III.—The Catholic Apostolic Roman religion is that of the State. The nation obliges itself to maintain the worship and its ministers. No person shall be molested in the territory of Spain for his *religious opinions*, nor for the exercise of his *particular worship*, saving the respect due to Christian morality. Nevertheless, *no other ceremonies nor manifestations in public* will be permitted than those of the religion of the State.

Such is the Constitution which is to govern the administrators of the law. But the law is to be construed, and it is possible to give such construction to the words "particular worship" and "no other ceremonies nor manifestations in public," as will preclude any worship by Protestants except in private houses. The High Church party in Spain hold that under this article of the Constitution no house for public worship can be opened, no books hawked about the streets, no signs put on churches or bookstores, and no schools allowed. This is extreme and partisan construction. At the request of the English government, the distinguished lawyer and statesman who drafted this article in the Constitution, Martinez, has given a long and learned opinion upon it, which I was permitted to read in manuscript. He holds that no interference can be made with worship within any house or within a cemetery, but that the sale of books, Bibles and tracts, posting notices of public worship, signs on churches or depositaries for the sale of books, can be regulated by law, and, until such laws are passed, the government is to construe the Constitution and carry it into effect.

CHRISTIAN AMUSEMENTS.

Madrid is for the most part built like Paris. Families live in flats, with little appearance of comfort by way of furniture or convenience. They are very economical, and never entertain by giving dinners. At evening parties no refreshments are given excepting tea and coffee, and certain sweetened drinks. The streets of the city are generally regular and well built. They radiate from the central square, Puerto del Sol, or the Gate of the Sun, because it was formerly the eastern gate of the city.

It is now the centre around which are built the hotels and the large cafés. On the eastern side of the city is the Prado or meadow, which is the great boulevard of Madrid, where all the fashion and wealth displays itself in the summer evenings. It is composed of wide avenues for driving, and sidewalks for lounging and sitting, about two and a half miles in length, and planted with trees. The trees are connected by trenches, and a small depression is made around each for the purpose of artificial irrigation. The climate is so dry that no trees will grow without being watered. To the east connected with the Prado, is a park for driving and walking, called Bueno Retiro. It is filled with trees and shrubbery, with preparations for artificial irrigation. But there is no lawn or grass to be seen. I have never seen a field of grass in Spain. The hot, dry summer destroys it. There is no hay for horses and cattle. They are fed on straw and grain. To the east of this park lies the bull-ring. Every city in Spain has its bull-ring. The fights are generally held from April till October, and on Sunday after Church. The Church is obliged to give its countenance to the bloody sport by sending a priest with the consecrated host to remain in attendance in order to administer the sacrament in case one of the fighters is fatally injured. A doctor is also always present.

The bull-ring of Madrid is a new circular amphitheatre built of brick and stone, 300 feet in diameter, with twenty rows of stone seats, one above another. There is a central seat for the president of the ring, who is generally some gentleman or nobleman. There are also rows of private boxes, and a king's box.

The whole exhibition is under the direction of an association of distinguished citizens—usually noblemen—who appear in their uniforms of gaudy colors and gay costumes, which always delights the taste of the Spaniard. A large gate opens into the ring, which is approached by a wide way, which is connected with the various stalls of the bulls in the rear. Each bull is confined in a separate stall, with food and water let down to him from above. The stall is opened by ropes from above. There is a large yard in the rear, connected with the stalls, where the bulls are sometimes baited before the fight. The bulls intended for the ring are raised in the mountains of the western part of Spain and about Seville, which is the great centre of this sport. The bulls, when one year old, and while in pasture, are tried by the herdsman, who baits them and defies them with his long goad. If they show the white feather they are converted into oxen. In order to remove these dangerous animals from their pastures to the city where the fight is to be held, tame oxen are used to entice them to follow into cages or stalls, which are moved on wheels or taken on the railroad. In the same manner they are enticed by the tame oxen into the yard of the bull-ring. The bull-fight is attended by all classes, from the king to the peasant, very much as was the Roman amphitheatre. Some come to see nerve, agility and courage ; some to see and feel the tragedy of blood and death ; the ladies, who may not be supposed to be enticed by these repulsive features, come to see and to be seen—to display their fine faces and fine dresses. When a horse, disemboweled, dragging his intestines, his sides covered with blood, is careering around the ring, pursued and goaded by the bull, or when he falls quivering in his death agony—when the matador is goaded by his mad antagonist and thrown over his head, or the bull falls pierced to the heart—the ladies have only to shriek and put their fans before their faces until the bodies of horse, man or bull, are drawn out of the ring by the gay team of mules, always ready for the occasion.

The exhibition of each bull consists of three acts, all of which are performed in about twenty minutes. First, at a signal by the president, the door is thrown open, and the bull, dazed by the glare of the light, dashes into the ring. He sees the picadors drawn up on the right of the ring on horses, each rider having a long pole and a short sword. The bull makes for the first picador, whose skill is shown in turning his horse so as to shun the plunge of the bull or turn him away, or, failing to do this, to put his horse as a shield between himself and the bull. If the bull misses the first picador he dashes for the second, and so on. This act lasts only a few minutes, but in it many horses are killed by being disemboweled. The treatment of these poor animals is one of the most horrid features of the ring. They are blindfolded, and if only wounded, the wound is sewn up or stopped with tow, and they are again driven into the ring, until death ends their agonies. None but the poorest animals are used for the ring; but the cruelty is all the greater, as their means of defence becomes less. The bull is never killed by the picadors. If, however, he is a coward and will not charge, he is dispatched at once with all manner of hissing and derisive epithets from the crowd, who call him a *coward*, and nothing but a *cow*. The dogs are then set on him, grapple him by the nose and bring him down, when he is stabbed, or houghed—that is, the cords of his hind legs are cut with a long knife and he is then drawn out bleeding and dying. If the bull is a brave animal, after a few minutes' contest with the picador, the second act begins. At a signal from the president, the trumpet sounds and a body of young men, called chulos, or merry-makers, enter the arena gayly dressed and with colored cloaks. They flaunt these in the face of the bull and entice him away from the picadors. They are exceedingly dexterous and skilful in escaping from the plunge of the infuriated animal. I was told by a gentleman that he had seen them, when the bull was rushing on them, leap between his horns and over his back. They will, as they spring one side of him, fix a little goad with a colored ribbon attached into his neck, one on each side and exactly opposite each other.

The last trumpet announces the third act. The audience are impatient for the death scene. One of the meanest features of the whole exhibition is that, no matter how brave, skilful and noble the bull may have proved himself, or how much he has entitled himself to life by all laws of honor, yet he must die. There seems not to be a sentiment of true chivalry in the whole performance. Upon my suggestion of the unfairness of this treatment to a brave animal, I was answered that if the life of the bull was spared after a fight he would pine away and die; that the excitement of the ring or the heating of his blood, always killed him. The third act now follows. Upon the signal, the matador—the executioner, comes in alone. He is the man of science. On entering, he bows to the audience, throws his cap on the ground, and swears he will do his whole duty.

He has in his right hand a long, slender sword, and in his left a red flag. After enticing the bull, with the flag, to make a few plunges, at the proper moment, as he darts one side to let the bull pass, he strikes the fatal blow; if he is skilful he pierces him to the heart between the left shoulder and the blade, and so quickly is it done that he draws the slim blade without a drop of blood, brandishing it aloft, while the bull in his last plunge falls, the blood gushing from his nostrils, and dies without a struggle. The team of mules, with flags and bells, are now driven in, and the bull is drawn on a low hurdle around the ring, amid the shouts of the audience.

In one afternoon six or eight bulls are killed in this way. Frequently a picador or a matador will be gored and killed. He is then borne off to the priest, who has a room adjoining the ring, and there, forgotten by the noisy crowd, his soul is prepared for heaven, and he passes from the bull-fight to paradise. Such is a bull-fight, the Christian amusement of Catholic Spain. There are more than one hundred bull-rings in the kingdom.

It is the national amusement, and the great feasts of the Church and national holidays are signalized by them. It is not true that they are becoming unpopular, and that none but the lower classes attend them. The rings are among the finest erections in every large city, are under the direction of the best citizens, and have all the prestige of a fashionable display.

Bull-fights originated with the Moors of Spain. But in their inception there was some good reason for them. Cavaliers, with fine horses and a long spear, showed their skill and trained themselves by this practice for higher feats of arms. Now the amusement is degraded to gratifying a taste for blood, and is in the hands of performers who are in social life on a par with our prize-fighters and the professional bully. Centuries ago the tender-hearted Queen Isabella, failing to abolish this national amusement, sought to mitigate its ferocious character. She was so much horrified by one of these combats at Arevalo, that she refused ever again to attend a fight unless the horns of the bull were guarded, so as to prevent serious injury to horses and men.

Yet the Spaniard has his arguments by which he will defend this his national amusement, and it is fair to give him the advantage of them. He says every nation must have amusement, and a historical and traditional one, if otherwise good, is the best; that there is more or less cruelty in all national sports. The Englishmen and American will play with his fish and slowly drown him; will slaughter the buffalo for sport; hunt lions and elephants for amusement. They shoot pigeons and pheasants for the fun of killing them. Common people in all countries, with wives and children, attend executions.

All people are fond of the tragic—like to see anything and everything die game. We Spaniards in our day only indulge in the same propensities. We kill old horses outright rather than torture them in life. We kill bulls, which are used for beef, and in doing this we indulge our fondness for dexterity, courage and nerve. So reasons the Spaniard, and if we can justify ourselves it may not be difficult for him to defend bull-fights.

PARTIES AND POLITICS.

No one can understand the politics of Spain without some knowledge of the various parties and the form of the present government. Ferdinand VII died in 1833, having induced the Cortes to repeal the Salic law, so that females could sit on the throne. He had had four wives. His last wife was Christina of Naples. He was an old man, worn out by a sensual life, when he married her. He had had no children by his former wives. Christina was a far-seeing, unscrupulous, scheming woman. We must be pardoned for some gossip, which often contains truth and explains great public events. Queen Christina had two children—daughters. There are those who say, with much appearance of truth, that these daughters were not the children of Ferdinand VII. After the death of Ferdinand, the Queen was found to have secretly adopted another husband, with whom she is now living and by whom she has a large family. There is much reason to believe that no drop of the blood of Ferdinand runs in the veins of Queen Isabella. She began her reign, while an infant, in 1833,—her mother, ex-Queen Christina, being Regent. The character of the daughter was no fairer in after years than that of her mother. She married her cousin in 1846. He has always been considered a weak, infirm man. No children were born to her until five years after her marriage when a sister of the present King was born. It is common fame in Spain that Queen Isabella is a woman of loose life. Had not the crown been on her head, no virtuous woman would have endured her presence.

These things will account for the low estimation in which the people of Spain, of all orders, hold the Royal family. Domestic virtue has never been a quality of the monarchs of Spain, male or female, from the time of Ferdinand and Isabella. Ferdinand, even, had his mistresses. Charles V had his natural son, Don John of Austria, the hero of Lepanto. Philip II had his favorite, the Princess of Eboli. The life of every monarch since would reveal a state of morals truly deplorable. Purity of character in private life is not the commonest virtue among the men or women of the higher classes in Spain. It is far more common among the peasantry, who have felt less the demoralizing influences of religion, the Inquisition, and foreign gold, for the last three centuries, than the grandees.

DECLINE OF ROYALTY.

Thus it happens that this line of monarchs, once such absolute tyrants over a people their willing subjects, have now lost all hold on their affections and the prestige which royal descent gives in other nations. The Spanish people now use royalty only as a convenience, or necessary evil. Even Spain could not endure such a Queen as Isabella II. They banished her in 1868, and Marshal Serrano was chosen Regent till 1869, when Amadeus was elected King under a new Constitution. Marshal Prim was the moving spirit in all this. It was for the interest of the old line of the kings that he should be put out of the way, and he was accordingly assassinated in his carriage as he was driving from the Cortes. Amadeus arrived to attend the funeral of the man who put him on the throne and the only man who could keep him there. Amadeus was young, unfit for public business, with no character for stormy times and no appreciation of his situation. He hated all the duties of his station and neglected them. By his disregard of ceremony he offended the high and sensitive notions of the Spaniards and the foreign Embassadors. He would receive these gentlemen in his hunting-jacket and high-top boots. He left in 1873, when a Republic was declared.

THE CORTES AND ITS PRESIDENTS.

The Cortes appointed one after another President during the year 1873. There was anarchy in every province. Barcelona set up for herself, and the Basque provinces declared for Don Carlos, the cousin of the present King, who would be rightful heir provided the Salic law were in force. After many Presidents had resigned, Castelar wished to try his hand at governing. He was declared President. He had been a writer and a theorist, and firmly believed in a Federal Republic, after the model of our own, as the only government for Spain. When he came to rule a turbulent, discontented people, he found none of the theories which he had advocated all his life would work. He had to give up, and violate every one of them, in despair. He settled the affair of the *Viginius* with America to avoid a war, while there was a moral certainty that Spain was in the right. When the

Cortes met in the latter part of 1874, after he had been in power a few months, they disapproved, on the first night of the session, of everything he had done. He offered to resign; and, while they were discussing this question, a General of the forces in Madrid sent a message by his adjutant to the Cortes that he thought they had fulfilled their mission and had better dissolve. This aroused the Cortes to great wrath, and they began to take measures to punish this officer, who assumed to control them. While this excited discussion was going on, the aide-de-camp again appeared, saying the General was desirous of an answer to his demand. Accidentally a pistol of one of his guards fell and went off. The whole Cortes, thinking an army was upon them, fled in dismay and never met again. The same night a proclamation was put forth from some one, no one knows from whom, that the Cortes was dissolved and Marshal Serrano would assume the control of the government, under the name of President. Thus between night and morning the government was changed, without any visible power, by a mere paper proclamation. Marshal Serrano ruled till 1875, when another Junta suddenly, between night and morning, proclaimed, in pretty much the same way, Queen Isabella's son, Alfonso XII, King of Spain, with Canovas at the head of the government.

We have mentioned these details to show the working of parties in Spain and methods of overturning the government. The politicians are divided into numerous parties, there being about five now in the Cortes. They have their names—the Conservatives, Moderates, Liberals, etc. At the time of our visit, Canovas had the leading of more than half of the Cortes. Castelar was at the head of one party, consisting of himself and one other, and one party had only himself as a follower. The object of parties in Spain is not a change of administration, as in England and America, but it is the *overthrow* of the government; their opposition is conspiracy, and they are plotting against each other constantly, not only for control of government, but for a new one, with new principles and a new Constitution. With such plotting and counterplotting going on, no one can tell what may happen tomorrow. Any Captain-General, under favorable circumstances, may overturn the government in a night. Every General in the army has perjured himself over and over again. Conspirators are not punished, for the party in power know they may at some time be conspirators themselves, and they treat each other leniently.

THE PRESENT GOVERNMENT.

The people are now heartily tired of revolutions

and they seem disposed to give the present King a fair trial. The Monarchists and Conservatives support him. Since his accession, a new Constitution has been adopted in place of the one of 1869. Some of the principal features of it are as follows: The law-making power is the Cortes, with the King. The Cortes is composed of a Senate and a Congress, with equal powers. Senators are of three classes— 1st, those in their own right, such as sons of kings, grandees who pay a certain amount of taxes, certain generals, bishops, etc.; 2d, Senators appointed by the Crown; 3d, Senators chosen by electors who pay a certain amount of taxes. The Congress is composed of Deputies chosen by electors in all the 49 provinces in proportion of one to every 50,000 inhabitants. They must be 25 years of age. The Deputies cannot hold State offices or have pensions or a salary. They must meet every year. The King can suspend the Congress at any time, but another must be elected within three months thereafter. The King appoints the President and Vice-President of the Senate from among its members. The King is not responsible, but his Ministers are, for all acts of government. He cannot marry without the approval of the Cortes. Don Alfonso XII is declared King, with succession to his children. The Ministers appear in either House. They consist of the President of the Council of Ministers, who is the Premier, and eight Ministers, each presiding over a separate department of the State.

In some respects, Spain resembles the federal government of the United States. There are 49 provinces, each of which has a provincial legislature and a civil government. Each province, by prescriptive right from time immemorial has certain local rights called fueros, which they have fought to preserve for centuries. They generally relate to freedom from taxation and privileges of that kind. These provincial assemblies have, like our States, certain rights guaranteed to them, and, like our States, they administer their own local laws and also such laws passed by the central government as they are subject to. The effort of the central government is to destroy all these fueros or prescriptive rights of the different provinces, so far as they render taxation and other burdens of the general government unequal, and to make the provincial legislatures merely administrators of the general laws of the Cortes.

AN ELECTIVE MONARCHY.

The Cortes of Spain presents one of the features of Constitutional government in all its history. This is the principle of self-government brought into Spain by the Goths long before any Parliament existed in England. It has been a bright, golden thread all through the history of Spain. This principle, almost destroyed by Charles V and his descendants, has again reasserted its authority and will yet be the salvation of Spain. Through all the history down to Charles V, the Cortes, composed of the three estates—the nobles, the clergy, and the representatives of the towns—insisted on their right to *clect* the King, and they demanded the oath from him. In Aragon, upon the election of a King, he was addressed by the President of the Council or Cortes, who remained covered, in these words: "We who each is as good as you, and who together are greater than you, make you our King on condition that you preserve our privileges and liberties; if not, no." Then they elected a Grand Justice, who was to be placed above the King and decide upon all disputes between Cortes and King. We never cease to admire this feature in Spanish history. It has been the very bulwark of their liberties, the one grand rock they have clung to when all other semblance of liberty has been swept away by kingly and clerical tyranny. From the time of Charles V to the time of Isabella II, despotic power, backed by the Church, has been trampling out every spark of liberty in Spain; but this old Gothic principle of Gothic independence—the Cortes—has at last saved the nation. What the nation now needs is a stable government, peace, and the education of the people.

THE LAW AND LAWYERS OF SPAIN.

In many respects the Government of Spain is federal, like that of the United States, subject to the Central Government of the King and Cortes. There are forty-nine provinces, with a provincial governor and legislature elected by the communes, of which we shall first speak. The commune is the unit of authority, and consists of electors, and as the people are mostly gathered in cities and towns, communes are confined to these. Every commune of at least sixty in number has a legislative body called ayuntiamento, consisting of from twenty-one to twenty-eight members, presided over by a president, called the alcalde. It is very similar to the municipal authority of our cities with the mayor at their head. In large towns and cities there are appointed assistant alcaldes. The entire municipal government, with authority to levy and collect taxes, and to preserve the peace, is vested in this ayuntiamento. The members are elected every two years.

Out of this communal representation, or ayuntiamento, springs the provincial parliament of each of the forty-nine provinces of Spain, the members of which are chosen by the ayuntiamentos.

The provincial parliaments are invested with certain political powers with which the Cortes cannot interfere except in cases where their action shall contravene some general law of the kingdom. A most interesting feature of the laws of Spain is the fueros, or the ancient rights and privileges belonging to different kingdoms, provinces, towns, and cities. For example, Biscay is free from conscription, taxes, and stamps; the King and Queen of Spain are only Lord and Lady of Biscay. These fueros the different provinces have always maintained with great tenacity, and they have always stood in the way of a strong central, consolidated government. It has been the past and is the present policy of the General Government to abolish the fueros and to bring the kingdom under one uniform code of laws, each part bearing the same burdens. Don Carlos is the champion of the party in the different provinces who hold to the ancient fueros. The laws as to real property, descent, and wills differ in each province. Primogeniture as to lands has been abolished, but not as to titles. This will be a death-blow to the aristocracy, as an aristocracy without property is a mere name. All transfers of real property mortgages and all deeds affecting real estate must be recorded in the same manner as in the United States. Foreigners can hold real estate, provided they register the same. Spain has more codes and more compiled law than any other kingdom, and it is worthy of note that her civil law and the administration of it has been far in advance of her politics.

There are no less than seven different codes or compilations of the laws of Spain, beginning with the Fuero Jusgo of the Goths, as early as the year 480. There is a commercial code in force in Spain very similar to the French code of 1807. Probably the earliest published code of mercantile law in the world was issued at Barcelona in 1494, called the *law of the sea.* It was the law of maritime Europe for centuries.

We are surprised to find what a large body of law has been published in Spain, and how much labor has been bestowed upon it by the jurists of the kingdom. Numerous faculties exist in the different universities for teaching and lecturing upon these codes, and all barristers must take a degree from some one of these faculties before they are admitted to the bar.

For the administration of justice the whole of Spain is divided into districts and circuits, very much as the United States are divided for federal courts.

1st. There is one supreme court of appeal of universal jurisdiction, which sits at Madrid. It has a chief president and three branches of eight judges each. It has jurisdiction of all cases in civil and criminal law, and has authority to prosecute various corporations, ecclesiastical and political, and to entertain writs of certiorari to other courts.

2d. Territorial courts, which have the same jurisdiction in their respective territories.

3d. Courts of the 1st instance, to hear certain classes of minor offences in each district.

4th. Municipal courts, similar to our justices' and mayors' courts, which take cognizance of cases not involving more than fifty dollars and petty offences.

There is a judicial officer, called justice of instruction, who investigates criminal cases and prepares them for trial. All the chief judges are appointed by the crown and receive a salary. There are various ecclesiastical courts and courts for the army and navy. There is a court to adjudicate claims against the government, and a special court for the trial of the newspaper press. The bar is divided into barristers and attorneys; no one can act in both capacities. The barrister must have received an academic education, and a degree of licentiate at law at a university. This degree is not required of the attorney.

Both judges and barristers are amenable to prossecution and fine for dereliction in duty. The judges and barristers are men of learning and ability and would do honor to the bar of any country. There is care enough and lawyers enough in Spain to save the country, and it is our opinion that if the nobility and the politicians were equal to the judges and the lawyers, the country would be redeemed. There is a jury sitting with the judge in criminal cases, and the attempt has been made recently to introduce the trial by jury in all civil cases. This has been strenuously resisted by the people themselves on the ground that they are not willing to give their time to settle other men's quarrels. They have not been educated to the jury system. It has not in their eyes the prestige of once having been the bulwark of the liberties of the people, and they take a common-sense view of it. For two good reasons they reject it when applied to civil matters. First, on the ground that substantial justice is more likely to be done by the decision of one wise judge accustomed to evidence than by that of twelve men not so accustomed; and, secondly, on the ground that twelve men should not be called to pay the penalty of a disagreement between two. Let us pay a visit to one of the courts. In the Calle de Atocha is the Audiencia, or the Supreme Court of Madrid and its district. It is in the old building which was once the Newgate of Madrid. This court corresponds to a Circuit Court of the United States. The court room is large and hung with red curtains. At one end, on a platform behind a table, sit six judges elderly and scholarly-looking men with black silk caps on their heads and wearing black gowns trimmed with gold lace around the wrists. Next to the judges' platform a portion of the room is railed off, within which seats with desks in front of them are provided for the barristers. No person except two barristers and the clerk are inside the railing. On the wall opposite the judges hangs a good picture of the crucifixion. This I found in every court room and was told it was a universal custom. At the time of my visit the barristers were arguing a case, and spoke sitting with large briefs before them, but with no law books. They were well dressed, spoke without wig or cap, with great fluency and earnestness. When the court had heard enough, the presiding judge rung a bell and said the argument was ended. Immediately the barristers gathered up their papers and bowing to the bench put on black caps and passed out. All the spectators are requested to retire and leave the judges sitting on the bench, who bow to them as they leave. The title of the chief judge has heretofore been *Regent* and he is by the new constitution a life senator. Among the barristers are many learned and eloquent men, such as Alvarez, Bugallal, de Muro, Martinez who drew the new constitution, Silvela Issasa, de Arriela Accirado and Cortina.

The civil laws of Spain have not been codified, but a commission has been appointed for this work and their report is now ready to be acted on. The criminal law is codified. The common law and the decrees of the Council of Trent form part of the common law of the country.

THE ESCORIAL.

Situate about thirty miles northwest from Madrid is the Escorial, which has been called the eighth wonder of the world. It owes its existence to superstition and is a monument of folly, but of folly of the sublime order, and is none the less interesting on that account. Charles V had directed, in his will, that a tomb worthy of his fame should be erected by his son, Philip II. On the 10th of August, 1557, Philip fought the battle of St. Quentin, with the French. This was St. Lawrence's day, who had been broiled about thirteen centuries before, at Huescar, in Spain—a martyr to the truth. In the midst of the battle of St. Quentin, when panic-stricken with fear, Philip raised his supplications to St. Lawrence—as did the warriors of old, when sore pressed, to Jupiter and Mars—and vowed, in case that saint should give the Spaniards the victory, to repay him by a monument worthy of the benefit bestowed. The Spaniards conquered. When his wars were over, Philip, in order to fulfill his vow and the directions of his father's will, to indulge his monkish propensities and his real taste for architecture and the arts, and as an excuse to withdraw himself from the cares of his court at Madrid, set himself, as the last act of his life, to build the Escorial. He was the chief architect, and in it he was to gratify his gloomy, ascetic nature, and build a fitting residence where he—half king, half monk—might end his days.

This great edifice he located at the foot of the lofty and barren mountains of Guadarama, which tower above it in grim and fitting grandeur. Instead of constructing a magnificent Gothic cathedral, embodying the religious sentiment of the age and of all ages, with a crypt for his royal father, and calling it St. Lawrence, he built this strange mixture of cathedral, palace, tomb and monastery—an incongruous mixture, where each part mars the effect of the other. In fulfillment of his vow, the pile was to be in the form of St. Lawrence's gridiron standing bottom upward. The four towers are the legs; the royal apartments are the handle; the temple and the cloisters fill up the framework and are built in lines across a large parallelogram, leaving courts within to represent the interstices of the holy instrument. It is 744 feet from north to south and 580 from east to west. It cost about fifty millions of dollars. It is built of dark granite, with no architectural ornament to relieve the externals. It has 11,000 windows, 80 staircases, 73 fountains, 1,860 rooms, and was intended rather for the convenience of the two hundred monks than for architectural effect. The windows are small and give the appearance of an immense factory. It was commenced in

1563 and finished in twenty-one years. Philip had the gloomy satisfaction of living in it as a monk and among the monks just fourteen years to a day thereafter.

It has a grand situation, elevated, buttressed against the lofty mountain which towers above it and far away in a broken line to the north; while on the other side the view over the plains below, toward Madrid, is extensive and impressive. Stretching from the walls to the plain below are gardens filled with ponds and fountains and laid out in the stiff French style.

A hurried walk through this immense pile would consume a whole day. The cloisters of the monks would be of no interest. The palace for the residence of the royal family is the usual wilderness of rooms, suite after suite, filled with gilded furniture of silk and satin. The best pictures have been carried to Madrid and now are in the Museo. There is one thing, however, in these royal apartments worthy of note. There is a most magnificent array of tapestry, apparently Gobelin, filling room after room and suite after suite; it would seem almost a mile in extent. The walls of the rooms are entirely covered with it. Here are the rooms of Don Carlos, the unfortunate son of Philip, who is said to have fallen in love with his mother-in-law, the queen. He hated his father and was hated by him in return, and Philip is said, but not on good authority, to have put his ill-fated son to death secretly.

The Temple, as it is called, is the best part of the Escorial. It is 320 feet long, 230 feet wide, and the top of the dome over the centre 320 feet high. There are three lofty naves stretching from end to end, without any object in the centre to break the view. The coro, or choir, which is usually in the centre of the cathedral, a position which destroys the effect the immense size ought to produce, is here put at one end, in a gallery over the grand front entrance. This entrance is closed by massive doors, which are never opened except to receive a royal personage, dead or alive. The columns are very massive, four of them support the central dome, which stretches up grandly, like St. Peter's, 320 feet. These four central columns are pentagonal and are about 30 feet in circumference. At the end opposite the choir is the high altar, which is approached by red marble steps extending across the whole church. There is over the high altar a gilded tabernacle, which has been erected in place of one of bronze covered with gold, which was a marvel of beauty and was destroyed by French soldiers, who took it for gold. It was considered one of the finest works of art in the world. The screen behind the high altar is 93 feet high, and is one mass of beautiful gilded ornaments, carving, statuary, and of all kinds of marble and orders of architecture. The roof of the whole Temple is frescoed, and the bright blue coloring stands out in pleasing contrast with the severe simplicity of all other parts. The proportions of the whole are perfect, and the impression, as the eye wanders from one end to the other, through these massive aisles and up through the lofty naves, is one of severe grandeur.

Adjoining the grand altar and opening upon it by a door is a small chamber, where Philip died. He was accustomed to live in one of the monk's cells above; but when he became too weak to attend the services and death approached, he was brought down into this little chamber, in order that his dying eyes might, with their last gaze, rest on the host on the altar. His death is thus described by Ford:

"His lingering end was terrific in body and mind. He lay long, like Job, on a dunghill of his own filth, consumed for fifty-three days, like Herod, by self-engendered vermin. The crucifix he held in his hand when he died was the same with which Charles V had expired. He was haunted with doubts whether his bloody bigotry—the supposed merit of his life—was not, after all, a damning crime. His ambition over, a ray of common sense taught him to fear that a Moloch persecution breathed little of the spirit of Christianity."

Thus died the man whose minions under the

Duke of Alva had carried fire and sword over the Netherlands; who by the same instrument had planned with Catherine de Medici the hideous massacre of St. Bartholomew; who had used the cells, the rack and fire of the Inquisition, in the name of religion, to gratify the cruel superstition of his nature.

At the right of the high altar is the *Relicario*, where this great gatherer of relics kept the precious treasury of dead men's bones. He had here 7421 relics, among which were eleven whole bodies, 300 heads, more than 600 legs and arms, 346 veins, and 1,400 pieces of teeth, toes, etc. They were kept in beautiful plated shrines until the French tumbled them out promiscuously, and they have since been difficult to label.

The tomb of the kings of Spain is a room beneath the high altar. You descend by polished marble steps, carrying a light before you, and are ushered into a room, octagon in shape, about forty feet in circumference, and about the same in height. All is cold, black marble around you. Urns of polished marble stand in rows around. The monarch who dies reigning is placed on one side and the consorts on the other. The line of dead monarchs here begins with Charles V and ends with Ferdinand VII, the reputed father of the ex-Queen Isabella. Here stand many empty urns, which time is sure to fill, unless republicanism shall break the royal line of kings. The monarchs who precede Charles V lie buried in different capitals in Spain. The great St. Ferdinand at Seville; Ferdinand and Isabella, and their daughter, Crazy Jane, mother of Charles V, at Grenada. Charles having abdicated in favor of Philip, in 1557 went to Yuste, and lived the life of a hermit till September 21, 1558, when he died and was there buried and remained for sixteen years, when he was removed to the Escorial.

He inherited a strain of insanity from his mother, and transmitted it to his son Philip. The lesson is impressive to stand in this dimly-lighted, sombre tomb, and see before you all that remains of monarchs who once ruled over the fairest parts of Europe and the New World, from the Danube to the Pacific ocean.

The French took from the Escorial all the silver and gold ornaments, but they could not carry away the massive granite of its walls, and so they have done comparatively little injury.

The pictures of the Escorial were removed in time to save them, and now they grace the walls of the Museo at Madrid. Among these were Raphael's *Pearl* and the Gloria of Titian, under which Charles V lay buried sixteen years at Yuste. In the time of Philip the cloisters of the Escorial contained two hundred monks, and Philip had his place among them. His stall is shown in the coro, where he chanted vespers with the monks, and where he was kneeling when he received, without a smile, the news of the battle of Lepanto, fought by his natural brother, Don John of Austria, and which saved Christendom from the infidel. The monks were disbanded in 1836, and now parts of this immense pile are used for schools. Let us state the fact fairly and leave the reader to judge whether the national religion has elevated or debased the morals of the people, has been a friend or an enemy to all true progress.

TOLEDO.

ABOUT fifty-five miles south of Madrid lies Toledo, once the city of kings and priests. The Goths, the Moors, and the Christians in turn made it their capital, and embellished and defended it. It lies on the River Tagus. In approaching it, coming from Madrid, we strike the Tagus sixteen miles above Toledo, and follow the river down through a fine valley, which in any other land would be a garden of fruitfulness. But the route from Madrid is through treeless plains, apparently barren. The soil is good for grain, but cultivation is miserable; no farm houses, no pastures, no cattle, no orchards, no grass are seen.

As we approach Toledo it stands forth grandly, a city set upon a hill. It is situated on the northern end of a high, rocky knoll, jutting out from the hills, which extend far away to the south, rising as they recede, till they reach the mountains of Toledo. On the north side these hills break abruptly down into a beautiful plain, over which hangs the city.

The Tagus, which is a fine, large river, coming from the east, strikes this line of hills near their northern terminus and breaks through them. Following a depression in the hills, it has cut a deep channel through them in the shape of a horse-shoe, and emerges on the western side. It entirely separates the northern end of this rocky promontory from the hills behind to the south.

Upon this hill, thus separated from the others by the river on three sides, and with a beautiful plain stretching away to the north, on the other, is situated Toledo. It was evidently chosen for the ease with which it could be defended. The river, which separates it on the east, south, and west from the hills behind, forces its way through a rocky, wild, romantic gorge, hundreds of feet below the city. Along the northern side of the city, facing the plain, across this bend, from the river above to the river below, a lofty wall with heavy battlements is built, looking proudly on all the plain below. The city was thus completely defended on three sides by the deep gorge of the river, and on the other, at the open end of the horse-shoe, by walls and battlements. Like Constantinople, it is far more impressive viewed at a distance than from within.

We cross the Tagus, into the city, on the massive arches of an old Roman bridge. It is a grand old structure even now. It has two wide spans, and is called the Puerte de Alcantara, or the Bridge of the Bridge. The view down the wild gorge of the river, with the rocky face of the mountain on one side, and the heights of the city, crowned with the castle, churches, and lofty buildings, on the other, is one of the finest city views in the world. To get from the river into the city we are obliged to ascend by a long, zigzag road, passing through the ancient walls by a lofty gateway built by the Goths.

THE PLAZA AND THE PEOPLE.

This leads us into the square called the Zocodover, which is the only open place in the city where the inhabitants can walk for exercise. It is only 300 feet square. Here the bull-fights and the *autos da fé* were held in former times; and here now, in the afternoon, the people walk up and down in their long cloaks, the upper classes on one side, and the common people on the other. There is an air of haughty gentility about the Toledoans, as if they were conscious of high descent. Although clothed in rags, which are covered by his long cloak, almost every Spaniard claims noble blood in his veins. He is poor, yet haughty and proud. In cathedrals, churches, palaces, galleries, in every public office or building, the officers will accept politely a little silver for their services. Beggars abound in almost all cities in Spain, and in Toledo particularly they are a nuisance. The cathedrals are filled with them. Toledo once had 200,000 inhabitants; it now has 17,000. The streets of the city are irregular, too narrow for a carriage, winding in all directions, up hill and down, and so confused that no stranger can find his way through them. The houses are tall, and the streets between them look like foot-paths and are filled with all sorts of filth. Houses and streets seem to have been built for the twofold object of keeping out enemies and the heat.

PAST GLORIES.

Toledo was once the capital of the Goths. Here reigned Roderick, the last of the Goths; and here, on the river banks, they will show you the baths where he became enamored of the daughter of Count Julian, whose romantic and sad story ended in the subjugation of all Spain by the Moors and the death of Roderick. Here dwelt Charles V in all his magnificence in the Alcazar, the great palace and castle of the city. Here lived also Philip II, who adorned the city with churches. Here ruled in princely magnificence the cardinals of Spain; among them Mendoza, who, in the time of Ferdinand and Isabella, was called the Third King, and Ximenes, one of the most distinguished characters of Spanish history. Here is the most magnificent cathedral of Spain—not so large as the cathedral of Seville, but far more artistic and grand; not more beautiful or perfect in its plan than that of Burgos, but larger and more elegantly finished.

The Archbishop of Toledo is still the primate of all Spain. Madrid belongs to his see. But the glory has departed from this once-renowned city. Decay is written on all its buildings, walls, battlements, churches, monasteries, and even on the faces of the people. It had once 30 churches and chapels gathered around the cathedral, 14 convents, 23 nunneries and colleges, and 9 hospitals. These buildings were large, and were erected high up on the walls of the city, in conspicuous places; but now most of the nunneries and monasteries are closed, and the buildings are tumbling to ruins.

MANNERS AND CUSTOMS.

Toledo has no business; scarcely a person is seen in the streets, excepting priests and women. The cathedral, with its priests and attendants, seems to be the only business place in the city, and the only visible means of support to the town. There are no hotels worthy of the name, no wells, no cisterns or water in the place. Water is brought up from the Tagus on the backs of men or donkeys and sold in jugs. We can easily imagine that cleanliness is not a fault among Spaniards. They will drink water all day long. It is sold at all the places of resort and at railway stations by women. Even at midnight, when the train stops, you hear the shrill cry, "Agua! agua!" But the use of water stops here. The

Spaniard never uses water externally. The clergy used to teach that cleanliness was a sinful indulgence, and Southey states that Saint Eufraxia entered into a convent of 130 nuns, not one of whom had ever washed her feet, and the very mention of a bath was abomination. Isabel, the daughter of Philip II, vowed she would not change her shift until Ostend was taken. The siege lasted three years, and the garment attained the tawny color which was afterward called and is now known as Isabel. Since the monks have been driven out, it is right to say the Spanish ladies have not considered personal cleanliness and moral purity so antagonistic as they once did. At Toledo the Moors once had water-works on the Tagus, with immense wheels, which pumped water into the city, but the Spaniards, centuries ago, allowed them to go to decay, and now, with the swift-flowing Tagus at their feet, the whole city buys its supply of water from the earthen jars.

Madrid and Malaga are the only cities in Spain that we remember which are well supplied with water; but there is not enterprise enough, even in these cities, to supply the dwellings with it. No Spanish house, inn, or hotel has any external conveniences, no yards or open spaces in the rear. With no water or drainage, the house is the receptacle of all vileness, and in Toledo is this the case above all other places. In order to endure the house one night we were obliged to hire the parlor of the inn and have a bed put in it as far away as possible from the intolerable smells, and sleep with the window open to the street.

Next to the cathedral and the Alcazar, one of the most interesting relics of this dilapidated city is the

FRANCISCAN CONVENT,

called San Juan de los Reyes, built by Ferdinand and Isabella in commemoration of a great victory at Toro. It has a commanding situation on the southwest side of the city, high over the gorge of the Tagus and looking far down its winding valley. It has been one of the finest specimens of the Gothic style in the world, and though for centuries it has suffered by the hands of the invader, particularly the French, still there are beautiful gems seen in the old rambling buildings, in stairways, balustrades, arches and windows. These bits left here and there show that once it was erected after the most florid style of Gothic architecture. Cardinal Ximenes lived here with his reformed monks. The outer walls of the church are hung with long ancient and rusty chains of immense size, which were taken from the Christian captives rescued from the dungeons of Ronda when that fortress was taken from the Moors in 1485. Here they have hung for centuries as a votive offering to the Virgin Mother.

To see Toledo properly we must go around it and through it. If we walk around it outside of the walls, from the river above the city to the river below we see its lofty position, and we see also along on its walls immense monasteries, nunneries and churches, deserted and going to ruin. The walk up through the gorge of the river is exceedingly romantic. There are along the banks many ancient mills, which have existed from the time of the Moors without any change. The bed of the river is so deep that scarcely anything of the town can be seen from its banks. As you walk through the city the silence is oppressive. It is the city of the past. You see a few women going to church, many priests in broad-brimmed hats and black flowing robes, and now and then a soldier and a water-peddler. There is no life, no business, no vehicles. But still all is so ancient, so singular, so confused, that you are constantly interested. You can trace in the old walls and in the buildings the successive works of Goths, Romans, Moors and Christians. To the artist this old, dead city must be a perfect treasure. Curious gems of Gothic, Moorish and Christian architecture meet you at every turn, in old doors, windows, towers, battlements, bastions, arches and bridges. All these are so located and combined with the beautiful natural features as to make this decaying city of the past a perfect delight to the artistic eye. The only edifices which are of much present interest are

THE CATHEDRAL AND THE ALCAZAR.

Like most cathedrals in Spain, this is so closely surrounded by buildings that you can get no good view of it except from above. It has one fine and finished tower. The body of the cathedral has five naves, which are very stately and effective, and it is entirely surrounded by side chapels founded and named after some of the most distinguished persons in the history of the country. The north doors are of brass and most beautifully wrought, and almost equal to the famous doors of the baptistery of Florence made by Ghiberti. The south doors are very lofty and are made of carved wood. The cathedral is 404 feet long and 204 feet wide, and the roof is supported by 84 piers. The stained-glass windows are among the finest in Spain. The choir is in the centre of the church, and is one mass of most elaborately carved mahogany. In it there are about a hundred stalls for the clergy and the singers. The stalls are in two rows, one above another. The upper row is ornamented by scenes from Scripture history, from Adam down, carved in the wood. The lower row of seats is decorated by scenes from the life of Ferdinand and Isabella. This carving is in the very highest style of art.

The high altar to the very top of the nave is composed entirely of beautiful work in wood and marble.

This cathedral has also a famous Virgin made of black wood, very ancient. It seems to be a cardinal principle with Spaniards, that the older and the uglier the Virgin the more worthy is she of divine honors. What she lacks in beauty of person is supplied by tinsel, brocade, pearls, necklaces, rings and trinkets without number. Fancy how the lowly virgin of Nazareth or the suffering mother at Jerusalem would have looked decked out in all this trash! They have here also a slab of marble on which the Virgin, in one of her flights from heaven, once alighted. It is railed off from the crowd and cased in wood, but you may put your finger through the bars and touch it, as all the faithful do. The inscription in Latin before it is: " We will worship in the place where her feet once stood."

And so they do worship the Virgin Mary in this cathedral, as well as in all other parts of Spain. After visiting all the cathedrals of Spain, one cannot resist the conviction that the worship of the Virgin Mary, or rather of her image, is the religion of the country. It is a strong impulse of our nature to appeal to one of like passions with ourselves, of deep sympathy with us, who is supposed to have power to help and to save; and the priests of Rome have taken advantage of this quality to introduce the worship of the Virgin. The Catholic clergy have taught, for ages, that we get justice alone from Christ; that if we want mercy, love and sympathy, we must go to the Virgin Mary. It is thus, that this suffering, sympathizing mother of God has turned the hearts of a whole nation away from the worship of the God-man. They have kept in the background the great fact of revealed religion—that the Saviour of the world was at once the sympathizing, suffering man, bone of our bone, flesh of our flesh, and yet God over all. They do not direct the people to Him for sympathy, mercy and grace, as well as for divine aid. The acknowledgment of this one great truth—the mediation of the God-man—has given Protestantism its strongest hold on the minds of rational men; the neglect of it has led, in Catholic countries, to the worship of the Virgin Mary as its substitute.

The associations which cluster around this cathedral relate to some of the greatest characters of Spanish history. "The Archbishop of Toledo, by virtue of his office, Primate of Spain and Grand Chancellor of Castile, was esteemed, after the Pope, the highest ecclesiastical dignitary in Christendom." He was the Cardinal of Spain. His revenues were princely. He led into war a larger number of vassals than any other subject. He often ruled the kingdom as regent and led the armies. Here Mendoza and Ximenes sat on their archiepiscopal thrones and directed the destinies of Spain in the noblest era of its history. Here Mendoza lies buried in the same chapel with the ancient kings. The Pope and the King of Spain are Canons of Toledo, and the King is fined if he is absent from the services on a certain feast-day of each year.

The Alcazar is an immense structure, dating from the tenth century. Charles V repaired it and lived there. For hundreds of years it has been deserted by the royal family. It is now converted into a military college, where about 1,000 young men are being trained for service in the army by thirty-two professors. Most of them are sons of noblemen and they are a fine, manly-looking set of young men. Each wears a long blue overcoat, red pants, a glazed cap, and a sword dangling at his side. They are the only signs of life in this old, dead city. Every Sabbath they march through the city to the largest church, each with a musket, with the senior officer at the head of the column, and a fine band of music. They fill the whole body of the church. A company, with their muskets grounded, stand each side of the high altar with their commander in front of the altar. Mass is then said for about fifteen minutes, during which time the band plays the "King's March." The music reverberates grandly through the lofty arches and over the vast crowd. When the host is elevated, the music is changed to a minor key, and the whole body of cadets kneel, with their muskets glistening above their heads. All is over in twenty minutes, when to the sound of music they file out again and return through the winding streets, in military order, to the castle.

As I saw the ceremony, crowds of people attended to hear the music and see the sight, but no one— soldiers or spectators—gave any heed to the services. This ceremony well shows the relation of the people of Spain to the Church. They will go to the church on feast days or on great occasions, hear the music, kneel before the host, pray to the Virgin Mary, and cross themselves when they pass her image. Religion is a necessary form to the Spaniard, because he is educated to feel the power of the Church over him. It is convenient for him in sickness or old age.

There is only one thing about Toledo which reminds one of the nineteenth century. About a mile below the city, on the plain by the river Tagus, is situated the famous manufactory of

TOLEDO BLADES.

Here are made all those Spanish swords which are so famous for their polish, temper and beautiful workmanship. The works are in an immense rectangle, and employ hundreds of men. To the Spaniard this is the most wonderful object around Toledo. To us it was the least. To the Spaniard, whose eyes had ever been familiar with grand old cathedrals and ruins of bygone centuries, a manufactory was a marvel. To the American, whose ears are familiar with the sound of the spindle and triphammer, the rare works of ancient genius are the wonder.

We lingered on the walls of this old capital until the sun went down, casting its last gleams upon its lofty heights, upon the Alcazar and the proud old cathedral tower, and threw long shadows into the gorge of the Tagus. A kind of fascination held us here on the high ramparts of the eastern wall until the full moon arose and in turn threw its soft gleams on castle, and ramparts and far down into the valley of the river. It brought out in full relief the bastions and towers which stood, like grim sentinels, over the weird scene, mourning, if ought inanimate e'er mourns, over the departed glories of this once mighty city. They had looked down into these same valleys filled in turn with the legions of Rome, the swarms of the invading Goths, the armies of the fiery Moor and the hosts of Christian warriors. They had beheld the deeds and glory of Wamba, of Charles V, of Mendoza and Ximenes, men mighty in Church and State. They had beheld the bloody rack of the Inquisition and the fires of the *auto-da-fé*. They seemed to say: "All are gone—Romans, Goths, Moors, Emperors, Cardinals, with all their pomp and power,—while we remain. Man dies, but we live. He is mortal; we are immortal."

So reason the gloomy towers of Toledo by moonlight, as they watch over dead kings and cardinals. So reasons the man who knows no hereafter.

LA MANCHA.

MANY a lover of Don Quixote, or Don Quijote, as the Spaniards call him, would go to Spain for the sake of viewing the scenes where the famous knight and his doughty squire gained immortal renown. On our way from Toledo to Granada we pass through the province of La Mancha, which the genius of Cervantes alone could have made famous. It is a treeless country, its soil impregnated with salt, with a few squalid villages, with a race of poor but industrious people, of whom Sancho Panza is a good specimen. At Menzenares we are in the centre and in the capital of the province of La Mancha. Here we are within a few miles of the little inn, Venta de Quesada, where Don Quijote was knighted, and occasionally we pass one of those wind-mills or a flock of sheep which furnished an opportunity for the display of his martial prowess.

The peasants of Spain have the most implicit belief in the existence of this renowned knight. He is a reality to them. His marvelous adventures, and those of the Cid, are the great fund of song and story at the village inns of Spain. About fifty miles further on we reach the station of Baeza. Here there are mines of lead and copper, worked in the same manner as they were under the Romans two hundred years ago. Here Scipio the younger fought a great battle with Asdrubal, about 200 B. C. Here you may see the ruins of the palace of Himilce, the wife of Hannibal. But the crowning honor of this place is that it is the birth-place of St. Ursula, who so heroically ended her life at Cologne with her 11,000 virgins, whose bones we have many of us seen there. It is generally bad taste to spoil a good story, but I must be allowed the explanation of this legend given by Ford, which is that it arose from a mistaken reading of an old manuscript which was "Ursula et XI. M. V.," meaning eleven martyred virgins.

From Toledo to Granada our way runs nearly south, crossing the headwaters of the Guadiana and the Guadalquivir. We strike the latter at Menjibar, from whence it flows southwesterly to the Atlantic, passing in its course Cordova and Seville, two of the most beautiful cities in Spain. It is not the beautiful, clear, poetic river, sometimes described in song. In winter and spring it is swollen and turbid, cutting away its banks and overflowing them. In summer it dwindles to a shallow stream, winding through wide, treeless meadows.

ON THE DILIGENCE.

At Menjibar we leave the railroad, which is very circuitous in its route to Granada, for the diligence. If we wish to see real Spanish life, customs, dress, and the people as they live, we must take the diligence through the small villages, stopping at the posadas and ventas, as the village inns are called. On a fine day, with beautiful mountain scenery, mounted on the driver's seat, with six horses or mules, each having bells, the diligence is the very poetry of traveling. One postilion rides one of the leaders from eight in the morning till eleven o'clock at night,—eighty miles without a rest. It is said that these postilions, before the days of railroads, rode from Madrid to Granada, a journey of two hundred miles, in two days and a night. We had another attendant who seemed to be a conductor, and went the whole journey. Another, called the Mayoral, drove the team, having reins only for the wheel horses. He would drive only from one station, where horses were changed, to another, and always came with and left with his team, and had the entire charge of them in the stables and on the road. He carried with him a bag of stones, which he would throw with great skill at the leaders which his whip would not reach. The driver talked and shouted to the horses all the way, and at a certain sound made by him at the foot of a hill they would break into a run. About every eight miles, the driver, with his horses, would leave, and a new driver and a fresh team would take their places. The postilion carried a horn slung around his neck, with which he heralded our approach to every village.

Leaving Menjibar, we wind for a short distance along the banks of Guadalquivir, which we soon cross on an iron bridge, and make our way up out of the valley on to the high, treeless plains, which are bare and muddy in winter and hot and parched in summer.

THE SPANISH POLICE.

For fifteen miles we see not a tree, not a fence, not a field of grass, scarcely a house or a person, except the guards who patrol the roads. These guards civiles are stationed on most of the traveled routes of Spain, for protection against banditti. They are sometimes mounted and always well armed, dressed in military uniform, with a cocked hat. They are found at every railway station, in every village, and at regular distances upon all the roads. They are fine-looking men of good character. We found them miles away from any dwelling, two together, patroling the roads over which we passed, always armed with a musket. They have rendered traveling safe in all parts of Spain.

SIGHTS AND SMELLS.

A ride of fifteen miles over plains which have every appearance of barrenness, gradually rising, brings us to the ancient city of Jaen, which is beautifully situated among the hills. It is the key to Granada from the north; mountains rise around it in every direction. It has a cathedral, a number of fine churches and some famous relics. As we have no partiality for old bones, teeth, finger nails, locks of hair, or old rags, we spend no time upon them. Here we made our first trial at a venta, or country inn. As we were to travel till eleven o'clock at night without anything to eat, my guide brought me a most delicious morsel of veal, fried in vinegar and garlic, which, with bread, was all the venta afforded. We were contented with oranges and bread for our day's provision. Our fellow-travelers here provided themselves for the day—bread and sausages seasoned with garlic and fried in garlic. During a shower we were obliged to ride in the coupé, shut up with two of them. Every few minutes they would partake of the sausage and politely offer me some. After indulging in this food for some time they became thoroughly impregnated with the odor. They breathed garlic from within; their pockets emitted garlic from without. Garlic was everywhere. The air was filled with it; and such garlic who can describe? Shut up in the close coupé with these two persons the odor was terrific, and sea-sickness is a comfort to what I felt. I was obliged to open the window, put my head out and pretend to look at the beautiful scenery. At Jaen we are about fifty miles from Granada. Our road lies through winding valleys, along which mountain torrents rush in winter and the beds of which are often used as roads in summer. We ascend gradually through pass after pass, where, hand to hand, the Moors and the Christians fought over every inch four centuries ago. We are now among the Sierra Susanna, which bound the Vega of Granada on the north. Their lofty snow-capped heights look down into one of the most fruitful and lovely valleys under the sun.

THE APPROACH TO GRANADA.

As we emerge from the mountain valley and descend into the Vega, a new world bursts upon us. The flow of the waters, diverted from the mountain streams for irrigation, is everywhere heard like music. You exchange sterility for verdure of living green; the orange, lemon, and fig trees everywhere abound, filled with bloom or fruit; the air is fragrant with flowers; beautiful villas setting back from the road, surrounded by gardens, begin to appear.

Through this wealth of living verdure, the road, broad and lined with trees, makes its way up to Granada, like the approach to the city of a great king. The night is upon us before we reach the gates of the city. Two old Moorish towers frown from above the gates as we enter through the massive walls. We wind our way through the narrow and dimly-lighted streets until we reach the eastern side of the city, and ascend through a grand avenue of trees to the Hotel Washington Irving, which is just without the walls of the ancient fortress of the Alhambra.

ANNIVERSARY OF THE TAKING OF THE ALHAMBRA.

We arrived at the Hotel Washington Irving on the first day of January. Here Mr. Irving lived until he took up his abode in one of the rooms of the Alhambra, which he most graphically describes in his tales.

We were awakened on the morning of the second of January by the ringing of all the bells in the city below us, and by the bell on the tower of the Alhambra above us. The streets were filled with people shouting and laughing as if some grand occasion had dawned. We soon found that the 2d of January, 1492, was the day on which Ferdinand and Isabella received the keys of Granada from Boabdil, entered the gates of the Alhambra and planted their standard on its battlements after a weary siege of ten years. The great object of their lives was accomplished on that day. They had expelled the Moor, who for eight centuries had held the fairest portions of Spain. The Alhambra was the last stronghold. Internal dissensions among the Moors, and gunpowder and cannon on the part of the Christians, had done the work. It was a holy war, which enlisted the chivalry of Europe. The fighting Cardinal Mendoza was the first to plant the flag of Isabella upon the walls of the Alhambra. The second day of January has ever since been a gala day in Granada. It is their Fourth of July.

On this day there is a grand celebration at the cathedral in this city, after which all the people, from city and country, rich and poor, men, women, and children, soldiers, peasants, artisans, resort to the Alhambra, and spend the day in gayety and frolic. We followed the crowd early in the morning down from the hotel through a beautiful grove of elm trees—brought from England and presented by the Duke of Wellington—into the city and into the cathedral, not knowing what we were to see. Soon we heard music without and the moving of a crowd. Through the great doors the band filed into the cathedral, playing a grand march, followed by the Archbishop, clad in robes wrought in gold by Queen Isabella for the grand Cardinal Mendoza; after him came a long line of the clergy of the cathedral, covered with their sacerdotal vestments; then came the alcalde and the members of the city government; and, lastly, one of the seven captains-general of the army of Spain, with a company of soldiers completely armed and in splendid uniform.

The alcalde, or, as we would, say, the mayor, carried in his hands the ancient flag of Isabella, made of yellow silk, with the arms of Castile inwrought upon it. The grand procession, at the sound of martial music ringing through the lofty arches, marched down the great aisle to the high altar, the host being borne before it. The clergy advanced up to the platform on which the high altar stands, and which extends across the cathedral. They take their seats on each side of the altar; the alcalde, bearing the flag, also ascends the platform and stands before the high altar, without uncovering his head. After a short prayer and some incense, the procession, at the sound of music, preceded by the elevated host, before which every one kneels, enter by a side door from the cathedral into the chapel of Ferdinand and Isabella. This is a beautiful, large chapel, highly decorated, extending across one end of which is the high altar. Immediately in front of the high altar, and in the body of the chapel, stands the mausoleum of Ferdinand and Isabella, and of their daughter Crazy Jane and her husband, Philip the Handsome. Their tombs consist of a marble erection, most elegantly wrought, about six feet high, and large enough on the top for the recumbent statues of these four monarchs. The marble figures are said to be good portraits. Ferdinand looks treacherous and severe, as he was; and by his side, lies Isabella, looking serene, true, and pure, as she was. The faces of Crazy Jane and her inconstant husband are averted from each other. Underneath this mausoleum, in a little room below, lie the mortal remains of these illustrious personages. The procession comes filing in and passes the marble statues. The clergy proceed to the platform as before and take their seats; the alcalde and the civic authorities also ascend the platform; the alcalde hands the flag to the youngest of them; the music strikes up for a moment, and he, with his hat on, takes three steps forward toward the altar, on to the field cloth once used by Ferdinand and Isabella; he then waves the flag three times toward the altar; the music sounds again, and he waves the flag three times to the clergy; the music sounds again, and he turns and advances toward the dead king and queen lying in marble, and waves the flag, in solemn salute, slowly and solemnly three times toward them. It is a most impressive scene, the pageant is beautiful, the associations are inspiring. Drooping over the tombs are the battle flags of the warrior king and queen. The altar-cloths and priestly vestments made by Isabella, her missal, her sword, her crown and sceptre, made of gold and silver, her jewel box, are also in full sight on this day.

The procession then, in the same order, proceed to the cathedral again, where a short mass is said and a long oration pronounced by a priest. The crowd then make their way up the hill to the gate of the Alhambra. We follow them through the grand archway called the Gate of Justice. On the great horse-shoe arch above the gate is cut in stone the open hand as a talisman against the "evil eye," and on an inner arch below the hand is the key, the symbol of power. Through this grand gateway we are ushered into the great Plaza de los Albiges. The whole plateau of the Alhambra, all the halls, the courts, the gardens, and the tower, were filled with a crowd of people from the surrounding vega and the city, all dressed in the picturesque costumes of the country, and many of them peculiar to the city or village from which they came. All the ladies wore lace vails or mantillas on the head, and the peasants and poorer classes had silk handkerchiefs of bright colors. Not a bonnet was to be seen There was a band of music in one of the large plazas. There were stands for the sale of fruits, sweets, and water, but no wine was sold. There was no sign of drunkenness, all was hilarity, singing, and laughing. The great crowd seemed to delight in wandering through the courts, halls, chambers, baths, and towers of the Moorish palace. This is the only day of the year when water fills the fountains of the Alhambra. The little lakes in all the courts were glistening with the cool streams from the Sierra Nevada. The Fountain of Lions was throwing forth its streams from twelve open mouths. Everywhere there was a gentle murmur of falling waters. Amid these scenes the people, fond of the beautiful, with a taste for sensuous delight, wandered till sunset.

The point of greatest attraction seemed to be the Torre de la Vela, which is a tower overlooking the city on the extreme end of the Alhambra. The top of this tower is a large area one hundred feet square. On this tower, in the time of the Moors, hung the silver bell which was rung every five minutes during the night. It was heard for thirty miles across the Vega, and by it was regulated the distribution of water which irrigated all the lands. The silver bell has gone, but another is in its place. Every boy had to have a pull at the rope. Every maiden who rings this bell on this gala day is sure of a lover and a husband within a year. It is useless to say, its notes rang out one continuous peal from morn till dewy eve.

The day closed with an entertainment at the theatre, representing the taking of Granada. Here Ferdinand and Isabella, with their attendants and most renowned knights, all armed and mailed, appear on one side, and the Moorish warriors on the other. The Moor insults the Virgin and the Christians the Great Prophet, challenges are exchanged, and renowned knights engage in single combat. It ends with the delivery of the keys of Grenada by Boabdil to Isabella. It is a most absurd attempt to portray the scenes and characters of the great siege.

THE ALHAMBRA.

The Alhambra was to Granada what the Acropolis was to Athens, or rather what the Citadel is to Cairo. It was the castle to awe and defend the city, and also the palace of its kings. The leading characteristics of the Moors, who built it, were chivalry and sensuality. The Alhambra is but the outward expression of these two qualities. As the architecture which adorned the Acropolis was the expression of the taste and cultivation of the Athenians, and as the grand old cathedrals were the expression of the religious sentiments of awe, reverence and lofty conceptions of the pious devotees who erected them, so the Alhambra is the home of a warlike, voluptuous and cultivated race of kings. Like the great temple of Karnac, it was added to and beautified by each successive monarch, until it became one of the wonders of the world for its grace, beauty and extent.

The city of Granada has now about 75,000 inhabitants. Under the Moors it had 400,000. It lies at the east end of a valley or vega, which is thirty miles long and about twenty-five miles wide. The city is at the foot of the mountains, on the eastern side of this amphitheatre. The Alhambra is built on a spur of these mountains as they break down into the valley. It rises immediately over the city 350 feet. The hill is about one-half of a mile long, and in its broadest part 750 feet wide. It descends on three sides abruptly into the valley below.

The plateau is surrounded by a wall thirty feet high and six feet thick, which in some places is built up from the ravine below. The wall is not built of stone, but of gravel, tamped hard, with occasionally a course of flat tile. Sometimes a little lime is found mixed with the gravel, but generally there is none. The walls have now stood for six centuries, and though they are slowly crumbling away, yet they will stand in that climate for centuries to come. There is no stone work in all the walls, towers or palaces of the Alhambra. The plateau has been described in shape as like a grand piano, or a leg of mutton, with the apex toward the city. In the rear it joins itself to the rising hills, which stretch eastward and upward until they culminate in the snowy heights of the Sierra Nevada, 12,000 feet above the sea. Standing above the walls at different points were once fifteen or twenty large, square towers, each large enough for a prison, or the residence of a Sultana and her family, or a troop of soldiers. The French, in 1808, blew up eight of these.

If we ascend one of these, the Torre de la Vela, which rises directly over the city, on the very summit of the fortress, we shall get a magnificent view of the Alhambra, the city, the vega, and the surrounding mountains. As we look down on the Alhambra from this height we are surprised at the insignificant exterior of the buildings. They are all diminutive, most of them one story high, and none over two. The roof, covered with the pottery tile of the country, gives them the appearance of ordinary dwellings. This common and even shabby external appearance to buildings which are most gorgeously fitted within, is frequently seen in Eastern cities. The same thing will be noticed in Cairo and Damascus, where the approach to the finest residences is often through a barn-yard.

The western part of the Alhambra, looking down on the city, was devoted to barracks for soldiers and large squares for the exercising of troops, while the magazines and tanks for water were built underneath. This end of the Alhambra was separated from the grounds devoted to the royal residence by a high wall. There were formerly a winter and a summer palace, and numerous mosques and other buildings. Ferdinand and Isabella destroyed many of these to make room for churches and convents. The winter palace was destroyed by Charles V to make room for a grand palace for himself, which he commenced but never finished. It is about 200 feet square, built of white stone, overloaded with ornament. Before the roof was put on, the monarch's means failed, and subsequently an earthquake shattered its walls and gave it an ill omen.

The summer palace is left standing. But for centuries it was neglected and pillaged by every one, made a pen for sheep and goats, and a rendezvous for vagrants. Mr. Irving called the attention of the civilized world to this vandalism, and awakened the Spanish Government to save what was left of this monument of the taste, wealth and luxury of a once great nation. Now the Government have an agent here, Señor Contreras, who with great taste is engaged in slowly restoring the buildings to their former state. He is also making a private fortune by the sale of models. Those who buy had better pay for them when safely delivered in America. The summer palace which now remains is a series of low buildings built around patios or courts which are connected together by arches extending from one court to another. Some of these courts are large. The Court of the Myrtles is 150 feet by 80, and has a lake 30 feet long, filled with fish and surrounded by myrtles, cypress and orange trees.

The Court of Lions is 116 feet long by 66 feet wide, with the famous fountain of the twelve marble lions in the centre. Others are much smaller, filled with orange trees, flowers and fountains. Around these courts are corridors, beautifully paved, supported by small, graceful, palm-like marble pillars. Sometimes two or three columns stand together. Around the Court of Lions are 128 of these columns. Opening on these corridors and courts are the principal rooms of the palace, generally on the ground floor. The arched doorways, and the graceful columns supporting them, are each a picture of elegance. In many cases the eye catches a charming glimpse, through a long vista under arches supported by the palm-like columns, from one court to another and another, filled with flowers, trees and fountains. The exterior walls being six feet thick, the windows appear like port-holes. Often the view through them reveals a lovely picture of green hillsides, far across the valley and to the distant mountains.

Many large public rooms open on these various courts, such as the Hall of Judgment, the Hall of the Abencerrages, the Hall of the Two Sisters, the

Hall of the Ambassadors. Then there are the rooms of the harem, the baths, the mosque, the private rooms of the king and the boudoir of the Sultana. One of the most remarkable things about the Alhambra is the exquisite ornamentation of the rooms and corridors. The floors are of variegated tile, and each room wainscoted four feet from the floor with tile of the most brilliant colors. The ceilings are vaulted and covered entirely with stucco work of most beautiful patterns, among which are the stalactite and honey-comb patterns. This stucco work was put up in blocks, yet so perfectly done that no trace of the joining of the blocks can be seen. In the Hall of the Sisters there are 5,000 of these blocks used in the vaulted ceiling, yet after five centuries no imperfection can be seen, and it has the appearance of being one solid block of marble. These vaulted ceilings are exquisitely ornamented by colors of red, blue and gold, and all done with mathematical accuracy. The capitals on all the pillars were covered with gold, on red or blue ground. Grace and elegance are everywhere. Beauty is the genius of the place. There is nothing massive or solid but the exterior walls of the fortress. As it has been said, the Alhambra was made to keep heat and enemies out, and to keep women in, and every hall, every tower, every court, every boudoir has a tale of love or blood connected with it.

BOABDIL AND COLUMBUS.

There are a few places in the world where you can stand and read great events in the history of a nation with more vividness than the pen of any historian can describe them. The scenes of the nation's glory and shame are before your eyes. Such a place is the Acropolis at Athens; such a place is the Coliseum of Rome; such another is the Alhambra. As you stand on the tower of the citadel the most stirring and adventurous scenes of the siege of Granada are within view. The beautiful vega is before you, surrounded by mountains in every direction. The castles on their lofty peaks, and the defiles between them, have been the theatres of those thrilling adventures between Moor and Christian, so well described by our own countrymen—Irving and Prescott. This charming valley—one of the gems of Spain, and the Alhambra—the last stronghold of the Moor, were the prizes of their conflict. Standing on the tower you can see each of these at a glance. The grand amphitheatre, almost perfectly level, filled with groves of olives, figs and oranges; with beautiful villas rising here and there among them, is seen at a glance. The Darro, fed by the snows of the Sierra Nevada, meanders through the plain, and artificial irrigation, planned by the Moors, reaches every acre of land, bringing the waters from the mountain springs. Here they raise three and four crops annually.

This second day of January is the anniversary of the departure of Boabdil, the last of the Moorish kings, called by the Moors Boabdil the Unlucky. On the 2d of January, 1492, he, with his family and his mother, the famous Ayeshah, departed from this fortress of his forefathers. On the left, in the plain by the Darro, you will see the place where he gave up to Ferdinand and Isabella the keys of the Alhambra; and farther to the south the road winds to the top of a hill, which is called "The Last Sigh of the Moor." Here the dethroned monarch turned to view the fortress where his ancestors had lived for two hundred years, and the beautiful vega which they had held by their swords for eight centuries. As he took his last look at this paradise, the home of his fathers—as he saw the cross of the Christian floating over the walls of the Alhambra—as he was forever turning his face from them toward the sands of Africa—no wonder he wept. As he had lost it all by his folly, no wonder his mother reproached him, saying, "You do well to weep like a woman for that you did not defend like a man." Fallen like Lucifer, he turned from the paradise inherited from his ancestors, and purchased by their valor, to the arid deserts from whence they came eight centuries before. He died at Fez, in Morocco, killed in a skirmish between certain petty tribes. Some of his descendants are said to be beggars at the doors of the mosque in Fez at this day.

While the Moor was thus ascending the heights of the Alpujara, weeping as he went, there was another scene being enacted in the gorgeous Alhambra. Cardinal Mendoza had planted the standard of Isabella on the high walls. The great Gate of Justice was flung wide open, and the war-worn veterans of the Christian army, with Ferdinand and Isabella at their head, were filing through. King, queen, knights and soldiers range through these fairy-like halls, amazed at the magic beauty, such as their eyes had never seen. The great cardinal erects the altar in one of the beautiful corridors, and with the king and queen kneeling before him, solemn mass and thanksgiving to Almighty God is said for the great victory over the infidel, and that the mission of their lives is accomplished. But another scene was enacted in the Alhambra on this second day of January, 1492. Christopher Columbus, an Italian, an enthusiast, was in the court of the queen, and had been urging her to commission him, under her flag, to pass from the Pillars of Hercules across unknown seas to look for unknown lands and a way to the Indies. The thoughtful queen heard his arguments and was inclined to believe. But where was the money to come from? The ten years' war had exhausted her treasury.

Columbus turned slowly away, and next day departed to seek other aid. The queen could look out from the lofty Alhambra and trace his way across the vega. Hardly had he left, when her heart smote her. Like a woman, but a great woman, she changed her mind, and in so doing changed the destinies of the world. She sent a messenger in haste after Columbus to recall him. Standing on the Alhambra, about two leagues away, you can see a little hamlet called the Bridge of Pines, the scene of many a battle between Christian and infidel. Here the messenger overtook Columbus. He returned, and it is said that in the Hall of the Ambassadors, or, as some say, at Santa Fe, ten miles distant, the compact between him and the crown was signed, by which he was to bear the title of Admiral of Spain, become governor of all lands he should discover, and be entitled to one-tenth of all profits realized. The contract was shamefully broken by Ferdinand, and the great discoverer was allowed to die in poverty, if not disgrace. From whence were the means to defray the expense of this strange expedition to come?

Said the noble queen to her incredulous husband: "I will pawn my jewels to raise the funds." Isabella raised the money, but it cost the crown of Spain to discover America only eighteen thousand dollars. The box in which the jewels of the queen were kept is now at the cathedral in Granada. It is of silver, about one foot long, six inches high and six inches wide, with an oval top. It is beautifully ornamented with animals, vines and flowers, wrought in raised gold and silver-work. On this anniversary, the second of January, this box, with all her other personal effects, such as her flag, sword, prayer-book, are displayed in the royal chapel where she lies buried. For a few francs we were allowed to handle them with becoming reverence, especially the box, which once held the jewels offered to be pledged for the price of the New World. Looking down from this tower over the Alhambra, your mind goes forward for twelve years from the grand scenes above described. You see across the vega a sad and mournful train slowly approaching Granada. It winds its way up the heights and files through the gates of the Alhambra, bearing the body of the great Queen to this lofty fortress as her last resting-place. Twelve years more and you see another funeral cortège coming through the defiles of the distant mountains, bearing the remains of Ferdinand to rest beside his queen. The Alhambra, the scene of their greatest triumph, is now their tomb. They desired to be laid here to their final rest.

In their will a large sum was left to build a royal chapel to support its services, and to erect a mausoleum worthy of their fame. Their remains rested in the chapel of the Alhambra until the royal chapel and mausoleum were finished, when they were removed to the cathedral.

GRANADA.

The Alhambra, as a palace, was commenced in 1248, by Ibn l'ahmar. The word Alhambra means red, or light. Its walls and towers at a distance have a reddish appearance, and probably this fact was the origin of the name. It would accommodate forty thousand troops, with ample provision for water and stores for a long siege.

The Spaniards were profoundly thankful to the Duke of Wellington for his great services to them in driving Napoleon's troops from their borders. They wished to reward him, but without much cost to themselves. They therefore offered him the dilapidated fortress of the Alhambra. It would have been a fine thing for them had the Duke taken it and spent millions in restoring it. But the man who conquered at Waterloo was not to be taken at the Alhambra. He declined the generous offer. The Spaniards then most handsomely presented him with a magnificent estate on the Vega, about ten miles from Granada, called the Soto de Roma. It contains about four thousand acres of land, and its annual rental is about $25,000. This the Duke accepted, and the estate is now held by his family. Not accepting the gift of the Alhambra, he did the next best thing for it, he sent thousands of English elms to be planted in the gardens to the south of the walls. Here, nurtured by the springs from the mountains, they are now growing in great luxuriance. The road from Granada to the fortress winds up through them. As far as we have seen, this is the only grove of fine shade trees in all Spain. Hundreds of acres are embraced in this park of English elms. To one accustomed to the verdure and trees of America and England, this is a refreshing and charming spot, after traveling over the bare, brown and treeless plains of Central Spain, where you never see a field of grass, or a shade tree, and never hear the song of a bird.

Here in this park is a shady retreat from the heat of the sun. The sound of running waters is heard all the day long, and the song of the nightingale during the hours of the night. The climate of Granada, to one accustomed to the rigors of a northern climate, is charming. The burning heat of a southern latitude, which parches other parts of Spain, is here moderated by a high altitude of three thousand feet, and by proximity to the snow-clad tops of the Sierra Nevada.

In most seasons of the year, especially in winter, the air is balmy and bracing, and the clear azure above rivals the blue sky of Italy. The Vega is a marvel of fertility, is always green, always in bloom, and abounds in gardens and orchards, filled with oranges, figs, citron, pomegranates, and mulberry. Surrounded by such a country, Granada is therefore one of the most flourishing cities in Spain. The Moors and Jews have stamped a commercial character upon the city. One street, the Zacatin, is filled with Moorish shops or stalls, like a bazar in Cairo, where goldsmiths and silversmiths and dealers in silks and fancy articles display their wares. Here the Moorish doors, arches, windows and ornaments are seen in all the houses as they appeared four centuries ago.

The Cathedral of Granada, although comparatively modern, and a departure from the Gothic style, is a noble structure. It was commenced in 1529. Located in the city which witnessed the grand triumph of the Christian arms over the infidel, and the deliverance of Spain from a foreign foe, patronized by Charles V and Philip II, aided by gold of America and money extorted from exiled Moors and Jews, it was reared as a magnificent temple to the Virgin Mother, and as a final resting-place of Ferdinand and Isabella. There are five lofty naves over which the beautifully groined roof stretches, supported by massive piers, each composed of four Corinthian columns, united back to back.

A magnificent dome rises over the high altar, painted in white and gold, and in which are windows of colored glass, which throw down a soft light on the altar and coro below. Kneeling on each side of the high altar are the marble statues of Ferdinand and Isabella. Adorning the high altar are the works of Alonzo Cano, one of the brightest geniuses of Spain. His wood-carvings of sacred subjects are unsurpassed, especially those of the Crucifixion. He was also a great painter. On the walls over the high altar are some of his pictures, relating to the Virgin, the Annunciation, the Visitation. Granada was the home of Alonzo Cano. He was born here in 1601, died here in 1664, and lies buried under the coro in this cathedral. He obtained such celebrity in painting, sculpture and architecture, that he has been called the Michael Angelo of Spain. Almost every cathedral in Spain is adorned by some work of sculpture or painting from the hand of this great master.

But the gem of this cathedral is the royal chapel which adjoins it. A fund was left in the will of Ferdinand and Isabella for the support of this chapel, which is now invested in the lands of the Vega. On each side of the high altar are portraits of the king and queen, carved in wood, giving a good idea of their appearance and costumes; while back of their kneeling figures, carved also in wood, is a very curious representation of the conquest of Granada and the delivery of the keys by Boabdil. But the greatest attraction in this chapel is the grand marble mausoleum before the high altar. It is composed of two sepulchres side by side, on one of which, in life size, sleep Ferdinand and Isabella, and on the other their daughter Crazy Jane and her husband, Philip the Handsome. You may descend beneath these to the tomb below and stand beside the rude iron-bound coffins which contain all that remains of so much royalty. Here also is the coffin of Prince Miguel, the eldest son of Crazy Jane, and who, at the age of twelve years, was killed by a fall from his horse near Granada. There is a fascination about this little tomb. These five iron-bound coffins tell strange and varied tales of human greatness and human sorrow. Charles V standing over his grandparents, his parents, and his elder brother, said: "How small a place to contain so much greatness!" But all the greatness lies in the character of the great queen who rests here. Her reign is the brightest chapter in the history of Spain, and her name the brightest in the list of her rulers. She died far away at Medina del Campo, near Valladolid, but at her request they bore her here as her last resting-place. In the Museo at Madrid is a grand picture by Gogo of the drawing of the will of the queen on her death-bed. The king sits by her side, his long hair flowing on his shoulders; the notary sits at a desk before her; the clergy and her household are gathered around the foot of the bed. Bolstered up by pillows, Isabella lies, her pale face the picture of saintly resignation and queenly dignity, dictating her last, dying requests. To this little tomb, a few years since, came the ex-Queen Isabella. Here she said mass, here she opened the coffin of her renowned ancestor and gazed weeping on her face. Did she weep that the descendant of such an illustrious monarch inherited so little of her purity, dignity and glory? If so, well might she weep. If shame could ever mantle a woman's cheek, it would be here. While looking on the face of the embalmed dead, Queen Isabel II might well ask herself, What was she, and what am I?

ANDALUSIA.

Our route will now take us by rail to Cordova, which lies north-west of Granada about eighty miles, but by the railroad it is 140 miles. We go southwest about seventy miles in order to pass the Sierra Susanna, which hems in the Vega on the northerly side. Every foot of this famous valley has been fought over by Moor and Christian again and again. Here encamped the armies of Ferdinand and Isabella for years during the famous siege of Granada.

At Boabdilla we struck the road from Cordova

to Malaga, and from thence we go north about 80 miles to Cordova.

Andalusia embraces the south-western part of the Peninsula. Of all Spain this is the land of romance. In its climate, people and history, it differs from other parts of the country. Sheltered on the north from wintry winds by the lofty range of the Sierra Morena, and on the south by the mountains of Ronda from the burning blasts from Africa, its plains and valleys are the most charming and fruitful of all Spain. They abound in vines, olives, orange groves, and palms. Its shores are washed by the Atlantic, the Straits of Gibraltar and the Mediterranean. The Guadalquiver, the only navigable river in Spain, flows through a wide, rich valley. On its banks are Seville and Cordova, once cities of renown in learning and in the arts, delightful residences in winter, spring and autumn; while Ronda and Granada, high up in their mountain fastnesses, furnish a delightful retreat from the heats of summer. Gibraltar, Malaga and Cadiz are its seaports. Of all the Spaniards, the Andalusians are the most frank, openhearted, gallant and joyous. They are fond of amusement, poetry and the dance, and are in manners the opposite of the haughty and reserved Castilian. They are a gay, pleasure-loving, labor-hating race, thrusting all care from to-day upon to-morrow. They are the most picturesque in dress, most gallant and daring. The men are tall and well-formed, and the women of great symmetry and queenly bearing in their walk. Little labor is required for subsistence here. The climate is enervating, and so all the habits of the people seem to be directed to taking life in the easiest possible manner—to getting the most pleasure with the least work.

Our travels will take us by rail from Granada to Cordova, Seville, Cadiz, and from thence by sea through the Straits to Gibraltar and to Malaga. All these cities are Moorish in their general character.

CORDOVA.

Cordova is situated on the Guadalquiver, above navigation. It was once a famous Roman city, contended for by the armies of Cæsar and Pompey. Here were born the two Senecas and Lucan. Even then it was a city renowned for its high culture and intelligence. When the Moors, in 711, captured Spain, Cordova was made their capital. Under their rule it became a most renowned seat of learning, and the arts and sciences flourished here as nowhere else in Europe, in the ninth and tenth centuries. In 756 the Moors of Spain declared themselves independent of the kalif of Damascus, and proclaimed their own ruler kalif. It then contained about one million of inhabitants. Now it is an inland city, with forty-three thousand inhabitants, and dependent upon the surrounding country for its business, as no large vessels can come up the Guadalquiver higher than Seville. It lies in a rich, extensive valley, filled with groves of palm and olives, bounded by a high range of mountains on the north. I know of no place in Spain where you are not in close proximity to a range of mountains. The city is surrounded by old Moorish walls, and the high hills back of the city are crowned with monasteries standing out among the olive groves.

The Guadalquiver flows rapidly by the city, spanned by an old Roman bridge. The centre of attraction in Cordova now is the cathedral, which was once a Moorish mosque. It is almost the only structure left in Spain which has been saved from the reforming or destroying hand of Christians. This mosque was begun in 786. The builder followed the plan of the great mosque at Damascus. It was the third mosque as to sanctity in the world. It covers an area of 400 by 350 feet. Like most Eastern buildings, it is low, the roof, only 35 feet high, is almost flat, and is supported by 1,096 columns of all colors and sizes, of jasper, porphyry, verd-antique, and many varieties of beautiful marbles. The Moors obtained them by plundering other and distant cities in the same manner as the columns of St. Sophia at Constantinople were gathered from all the famous Grecian temples. These columns were brought from Nismes and Narbonne, in France; from Seville and Tarragona in Spain; from Carthage and other cities in Africa, and some from Constantinople. They all differ in size, length and color. As the Mohammedans had a passion for plundering other temples to adorn their own, uniformity was not considered.

The maksurah of the mosque, or the seat of the kalif, is still preserved, and also the beautifully-ornamented recess where the Koran was kept. The mosque is built within an immense inclosure, the walls of which are from thirty to sixty feet high and six feet thick. After passing this outer wall through a grand Moorish archway, you enter the Court of Oranges, filled with orange trees, having a large fountain and lake for ablution in the centre of it. Such a court is common to all mosques in the East. Across and beyond this court is the entrance to the cathedral. We must ascend the belfry tower, from which we have a grand view of the city, the distant mountains, and the river, stretching far away to the west through the green valley.

From this point you look down into the gardens of the city and into the courts of the houses, paved and filled with flowers and orange trees. The cathedral below you looks like a village of low buildings covered with tile, and gives no indication of the beauty within. One object in the distance attracts your attention. It is a massive bridge across the swift river. Its arches look a little irregular, for they have stood for twelve centuries on foundations laid in the swift current by the Romans. This cathedral is the finest and most complete specimen of Mohammedan architecture in Europe. But there is one thing to mar the unity of the grand structure. In 1623 the Bishop, Alonzo Manrique, not satisfied with the low roof of this immense mosque, attempted to add to it by building up from the centre a coro, grand in itself, and beautifully ornamented and rising into a lofty dome. Charles V well described this change when he said to the Bishop: "You have built here what you or any one might have built anywhere else; but you have destroyed what was unique in the world."

Seventy years were employed in building this coro. It has 109 stalls for the choir and clergy, and over every stall are most beautiful carvings in wood, illustrating Scripture scenes of the Old and New Testaments, beginning with Adam and Eve. The wood is mahogany, and some of the scenes have fifteen figures in relief, most exquisitely done. All the sides of this lofty coro are most elaborately wrought for fifty feet with life-size figures of the Saviour and the Virgin Mary exalted above all.

The immense number of columns ranged over this great space of 400 feet by 350 gives the singular appearance of aisles running in every direction They form nineteen longitudinal and twenty-nine transverse aisles, and look in the dim light like a forest of precious marbles, jasper and porphyry.

SEVILLE.

Of all the cities of Spain, Seville is the most attractive if we disregard historical associations. Built by the Moors, adapted to a warm climate and a life of ease, it retains all the characteristics of that luxurious people without signs of decay. Situated on the Guadalquiver, at the head of navigation, it has sufficient commerce to give to the inhabitants an air of activity and prosperity, and the advantages of business and wealth. There is an enterprise and life here which is seen nowhere else except in Barcelona and Malaga. Most of the streets are narrow and irregular, but well paved and cleanly, and the houses high. But modern ideas seem here to be gaining ground, for they are widening many of the streets and opening squares. Many fine carriages are seen, and good cabs can be hired. Along the river for two miles a magnificent stone quay is built twenty feet above low-water mark. And here may be seen steamers and ships from all parts of the world. In the winter freshets the river rises thirty or forty feet and overflows the whole country, and the city also. At the time of our visit it had rained twenty-four days successively, and we found boats ready for use in the public squares, and the doors of the houses opening on the street walled up for two feet to keep out the water which was expected to flood them. The city is circular, and a wall, about five miles in extent, surmounted by sixty-six towers, surrounds it, and separates it from the suburbs, which are laid out in beautiful gardens. Most of the houses were built by the Moors centuries ago. They are ornamented with pretty little bowers and windows, or little balconies, built out like bay windows, where a glimpse of the street may be had, and the cool evening air enjoyed.

They are invariably built around a patio or court, in the centre of which is a marble fountain surrounded by trees, plants, flowers and statuary. These courts are generally paved with marble and wainscoted for two or three feet high with the beautiful colored tile of different patterns. The front door of every house opens into a small vestibule, and between this vestibule and the court is an open-work iron door, so that you can look in to the court of every house from the street as you pass. The front door of every house is always open, and thus you have a succession of pretty pictures as you walk the street. The size of the court and the beauty of its decoration indicate the character of the house and the wealth of its occupant. The windows of the house, which open on the street, are protected by an iron railing, where the young ladies may safely sit during the evening and listen to the vows and protestations of their cloaked lovers in the street below.

The court is the parlor of the house. Here, in warm weather the family sit amid trees and flowers, and as their rooms all open on it, they take their siesta in the middle of the day, lulled to sleep by the music of the flowing fountains. This court is open to the sky. In summer they draw a covering over the top to keep out the sun and the hot air; otherwise the heat would be unendurable. Every story of the house has a gallery running around this court, and all the rooms open on this gallery and court. The lower stories of the house are occupied by the family in summer because they are cooler, the upper stories in the winter in order to escape the dampness. This court, which you see as you pass the door, this glimpse of flowing fountains, green trees, flowers, marbles and variegated tiling of all colors, gives a charm to every house and an air of poetry and romance to the whole city. Could it be always spring or autumn, Seville would be the most delightful of cities to live in. There is a happy joyousness about the people in contrast with the solemnity of the Toledoans.

Seville has always been the home of artists and

scholars. One of the largest universities and one of the finest libraries of Spain are located here. Here were born Velazquez and Murillo. The latter spent his life here, and some of his greatest works are still preserved here in the cathedral, the Museo and the Caridad. The most celebrated bull-fights are held here, and the finest animals for this national sport are raised near here. The bull-ring of Seville will accommodate 12,000 people, and the most skilful fighters are found here. The religious shows of Seville are unsurpassed, even by Rome. The processions in Holy Week and on saints' days are something unique. There is more of the imposing pageant of the Catholic Church, more superstitious reverence for the host and the images borne through the streets with great pomp and display, than in any other city of Europe. There are many semi-religious clubs of young men who join in these displays on holy days. The clergy of the city are numerous, of whom 132 are connected with the cathedral. Their vestments, wrought in gold, are marvels of richness and beauty.

The grandest pageants of the year are in Holy Week, when the whole city is given up to a holy revelry and religious jollity. During this week the host is borne through the streets attended by hundreds of the clergy in their splendid robes, blazing in gold and jewels. The host is placed in the celebrated Custodia, which is a silver tower formed after the model of the Giralda, the famous tower of the cathedral. It is of solid silver, about fourteen feet high, and weighs hundreds of pounds. This Custodia is borne through the city on the shoulders of men. It is then returned to the cathedral, where it is elevated on what is called the *Monumento*, which is an immense wooden structure or temple. in the form of a cross, which is, during Holy Week, erected on the pavement of the cathedral, over the grave of Ferdinand Columbus, the son of the discoverer. It reaches nearly to the arch of the nave. When thus erected and lighted up, with the lofty silver Custodia blazing at the top, and shedding its light on the thousands who crowd the aisles of this immense cathedral, the scene surpasses the wonders of fairy land.

SEVILLE CATHEDRAL.

Spain is noted for her magnificent cathedrals, but of them all, that of Seville is the grandest. A great cathedral is the highest conception of modern art, and the Catholic Church has the honor of erecting them in almost every country. The reflection has been made against Protestantism that it builds no great temples in honor of God. This is true; and it is also true that no more of these grand edifices will ever be built by Protestants or Catholics. The conditions necessary to produce them are gone from the world, never to return.

1st. Royal authority and royal revenues are not under the control of the clergy, as in past centuries.

2d. The clergy have not such princely incomes as they once had.

3d. The superstitious element, by which kings, priests and aristocracy sought to appease Divinity by the works of their hands, is wanting.

4th. Money, which in rude ages went for outward show into stone, marble, brass and painting, now is devoted to more practical good, such as hospitals, asylums, infirmaries, reformatories, universities, schools, churches, and the like.

The practical age has superseded the age of display, the age of reason that of superstitious devotion; consequently cathedrals—the outgrowth of this spirit—will never again be built. For this very reason they are all the more interesting to the practical men of the nineteenth century. These grand piles—the highest expressions of genius—are themselves storehouses of art. You must go again and again to them to get steeped with the impressions of their true grandeur, in the same manner as we need to see Niagara often, before we fully feel its sublimity. The mind cannot take it all in at once, so varied, vast and numerous are the objects which go to make up the grand whole.

Stand in the lofty doorway of one of these grand cathedrals; look through the great nave stretching before you 400 or 500 feet, between massive columns rising 200 or 300 feet above, till they are lost in the graceful arches above your head, as the trunk of a noble tree grows into the overhanging branches; see the soft rays of sunset shining through the gorgeous painted windows, and casting their brilliant colors on the marble pavement below; see the black-robed priests flitting like shadows before you in the dim light; hear the peal of the great organ, resounding through the lofty aisle; take in, if you can, all the rich fund of art—statuary, painting, carving—everywhere scattered in profusion through these vast spaces; fill your mind with the great associations which cluster here, the grand pageants which have come and gone, the mighty dead who sleep beneath its marble floors, and you have some faint idea of the impression of a great cathedral.

The cathedral of Seville is the richest and largest in Spain. It is built on the site of an ancient mosque, and on one side of a quadrilateral, which is 700 or 800 feet square, with a covered walk running entirely around it. Part of this square is occupied by a court filled with orange trees, with a fountain in the centre. Entering the quadrilateral and crossing this court, you enter the cathedral by lofty doors. The loftiness of the arches, the wide spaces and fine pavements remind you of St. Peter's. Solemn grandeur is the characteristic of this great temple. It is 431 feet long and 315 wide. It has seven aisles. The centre nave towers up 145 feet. The pavement is of black and white marble, and it alone cost, two centuries since, the sum of $155,000. The whole edifice is one mass of beautiful art work. It is lighted by ninety-three windows; many of them are elegantly painted and are 375 years old. The coro in the centre, open to the high altar, is one immense elaborate piece of wood-carving. The archiepiscopal throne is high above all other seats, and faces the high altar, with the seat of the Bishop on one side and of the Dean of the Chapter on the other.

Before the coro, under the pavement in the centre of the cathedral, is the grave of Ferdinand Columbus, the son of the great Admiral. A marble slab over his grave tells the deeds of his illustrious father and his own, and on each side are depicted the three little ships in which Columbus crossed the Atlantic. Ferdinand Columbus was himself a great traveler and writer, and gave a large library to the chapter of the cathedral, which can be seen. It contains many of the curious writings of his father. On the other side of the coro stands the beautiful bronze candlestick, 25 feet high, holding 13 candles. In Holy week, when the "Miserere" is sung, twelve of them are put out, representing the twelve Apostles who forsook him, and one left burning represents the Virgin. In Holy Week is lighted also the huge *font candle*, which is like a pillar of marble, 24 feet high, and weighs 800 pounds.

Twenty-eight or thirty lateral chapels surround the cathedral, each having its own altar, over which the Virgin presides. Many of them have beautiful pictures from some of the best of the Spanish artists. In the Royal chapel lies St. Ferdinand, the great warrior, who took Seville from the Moors in 1248, and who died in 1252. Over the high altar, in a most magnificent urn of gold and silver, lies his embalmed body. This great king is almost worshiped by the Sevillians. The urn is opened and the well-preserved body is displayed three times a year, when there is a grand military mass, such as we described as being observed at Granada the second day of January.

I saw more people in the cathedral at Seville, and more apparent devotion, than at any other place in Spain. One respectable man I saw walking on his knees across the cathedral to prostrate himself before the Virgin. He seemed well satisfied that he had done a good thing. One of the side chapels is devoted to the vestments of the cardinals, bishops and other clergy. There are two long rooms filled with them. They are worked in gold and silver thread and ornamented with gobelin. Some of them are

400 years old, and their splendor is something wonderful.

The cathedral is the great place of resort in Seville. Thousands might gather here and scarcely be noticed. Here, in the dark shadows of the lofty columns and in the long stretch of the dim aisles, is the trysting-place of lovers; here centre all the grand pageants of the different brotherhoods which parade the streets in Holy Week; and here beggars innumerable, on other days, as in all other cathedrals in Spain, hold sway.

THE GIRALDA.

Towers furnish some of the most effective architecture in the world. They are the glory of Cairo, as we look down upon it from the citadel on the Mokatam Hills. The Campanile of Giotto is the beauty of beautiful Florence. The Moorish tower called the Giralda is the beauty of beautiful Seville. It was built by the Moors in 1196, as a Muezzin tower, from which the faithful were called to prayer morning, noon and evening. It was attached to their mosque, which was destroyed by the Christian conquerors to make a place for the cathedrals, which it now adjoins. The Giralda was a sacred tower in the eyes of the Moors, and when Seville was taken they attempted to destroy it. But it was too beautiful an object to be lost to the world, so the Christian Monarch St. Ferdinand spared it, and it became a cathedral tower. It was originally 250 feet high, but a belfry of 100 feet more of open filigree work has been added, from which peals forth a chime of bells every hour of the day. Girdling this belfry is the appropriate motto in large letters of iron: "The name of the Lord is a strong tower." The Giralda is square at the base, and its lofty sides, as they stretch upward, present a succession of doorways and windows, spanned by the horseshoe arch; of balconies and turrets, all interspersed with the rich ornamentation in mathematical figures peculiar to the Arabs.

The ascent is by a succession of inclined planes within, winding around the four sides, making a wide, easy road, paved with brick to the belfry, so that a person could ascend on horseback. The ex-Queen Isabella, once ascended on the back of a donkey. The beautiful lattice-work belfry is surmounted by a figure of Faith, fourteen feet high, which serves as a vane, and she changes her position with the wind as easily as some people can change their faith. The Giralda, having stood for seven centuries, is still one of the most noble and perfect specimens of Moorish architecture in the world. We must ascend by its broad, easy road, 250 feet to its great bells, which have all been duly baptized and christened after distinguished saints. From here we look out upon one of the most beautiful panoramas any city in the world can present. Immediately below us lies the court of the great cathedral filled with orange trees, which was once the court of the great mosque. The domes, towers and roofs of the adjoining cathedral buildings, of themselves look like a small city encompassed by a lofty wall.

Outside of the cathedral grounds we look down into the open court of almost every house in the city, filled with trees, flowers and statuary, and adorned with colored tiling, each in itself a lovely picture. Around the densely crowded city stretches a wall overhung with trees, lined with gardens and surrounded by towers.

But beyond the city the eye takes in on every side a wide and beautiful landscape, bounded by lofty mountains on the horizon. Far away to the north-east stretches the Guadalquivir, whose valley is the garden of Andalusia. We saw it at its flood when it filled the wide valley for twenty miles in extent and ten miles in width, and had the appearance of a vast lake. To the east, far on the horizon, rose the snowy peaks of the mountains of Granada, where for two centuries the Moors had watched and threatened the kings of Spain in their capital at Seville. To the west of the city flows the swift current of the river, where at the quay are anchored the ships of all nations, and where once rode the navies of Cæsar. Across the river, to the northwest, about five miles away, is a little town seen through the olive groves, called Santi Ponce, where were born three Roman Emperors—Trajan, Adrian and Theodosius. It was built by Scipio Africanus. To the north, ten miles away, on the hills, lies Casteleja de la Cuesta, a small town where lived Hernando Cortes, the conqueror of Mexico, and where he died in 1547, neglected by his sovereigns. He died broken-hearted, as did Columbus. His body was removed from place to place, until at last it found a resting-place in Mexico, the scene of his conquests and his cruelties.

The objects of interest in Seville are numerous. There is here the Alcazar (the house of Cæsar), the royal palace, built on the site of the dwelling of the Roman Praetor by the great Moorish prince, Abdurrahm, in the tenth century. It has been changed and added to by every successive Christian monarch, until it is a mixture of Moorish and modern architecture of immense proportions. It abounds in patios, large and small, filled with lakes, fountains and gardens. Next to the Alhambra, it is the most interesting Moorish building in Spain. It is in perfect order, and was recently occupied by the ex-Queen Isabella and her family. The ex-Queen came from France with the promise that she should reside at Madrid. Her children, the king and his sister, could not endure her presence in the capital, and the Government was afraid she might again become the head of a party.

We should not leave Seville until we have paid a visit to the tobacco factory, which is outside the walls. The manufacture of cigars, cigarettes and snuff is a government monopoly, and they have large manufactories in different cities of Spain. This one at Seville is an immense structure, many stories high, with twenty-eight interior courts. It is about 700 feet long by 525 wide. It is surrounded by a moat and high walls, and guarded by soldiers. They employ here 5,000 women in the manufacture of cigars. These women are a class by themselves, like the Grisettes of Paris, and with much the same character. They earn from thirty to forty cents per day. They come all together like an army at a certain hour, and leave together also. They bring their food, their babies and their dogs. The babies are here fed, dressed and cared for, and are lying around promiscuously in all directions in this immense establishment. Each story looks like a tenement house for a thousand families. The women are not very attractive, but have a bold, staring, gypsy-like look, and an impertinent word for every stranger.

MURILLO.

We cannot leave Seville without doing homage to the memory of Murillo. Here he was born January 1, 1618; here he lived, here he gained immortality, and here he died, April 3, 1682. His genius pervades the whole city like an atmosphere. Here he founded an academy and school of painting. His works adorn the cathedral, the palace, the Museo, and almost every church. It is wonderful to see how the genius of one man, age after age, can inspire the minds of a whole people. His creations of beauty seem to live like sunlight in the minds of the people. What Raphael was and is to Italy, Murillo was and is to Spain. Both have been and will be worshiped as inspired geniuses—the one for breathing heavenly grace into earthly forms, and the other for transforming earthly nature into a divine loveliness.

The portraits of Murillo show him to have been a large, proud-looking man, with the bearing of a cavalier. He must have had some of the haughty imperiousness of the Spaniard. There is nothing of softness and tenderness in his face such as you will see in that of Raphael. He began life in poverty, and first painted pictures to be exported to South America for the churches. He married a lady of wealth, and thereafter he lived in affluence and entertained with elegance. He painted chiefly for the Capuchins, and his subjects are mostly sacred ones. His house, where he lived and died, still remains in Seville. In the south-eastern part of the city, close by the wall, not far from the cathedral and the Alcazar, he lived. It is difficult to find the house, hidden away in the Jewish quarter like the nest of a bird, as if to escape observation. But once there you feel the inspiration of the place. It has the usual Moorish court, which is filled with trees and flowers, with a fountain in the centre. The corridors are hung with pictures. Between the house and the city walls a large garden intervenes. On the second story is his studio, looking down into this court on one side, and on the other over the gardens and over the walls far away to the distant olive-clad hills. Here, in this little room, not more than fifteen feet square, surrounded by nature's beauties, worked and lived this great genius of Spain, among the creations of his own fancy.

Standing in this little room you ask yourself: Is it possible that here such creations as the "Immaculate Conception," "The Guardian Angel," "St. Francis and the Saviour" and "Moses Striking the Rock" could have been conceived; that here such glimpses of the divine and heavenly could have been caught and imprisoned by the canvas for the delight of coming ages. Indeed it is hard to believe that mere unaided human genius could have produced such ecstatic beauties as the pictures of Raphael and Murillo. Inspiration must have vouchsafed to them glimpses of the spiritual world.

The power to imagine and feel all the wonderful combination of forms, beauty, grace, color and feature which make up one of these pictures, and see them as a whole, and then to paint them as with the hand of an angel on the canvas, is to me superhuman. One of the most, perhaps *the* most, wonderful picture of Murillo, is the Guardian Angel, which hangs in the Sacristy of the cathedral. It is in his later Vaporoso style, with a soft, golden glow. The angel, with a sort of heavenly admiration and wonder, is looking down on the face of the Saviour-child, whom he is holding by his right hand, while with his left he is pointing to heaven, as if he were whispering some wondrous vision of that far-off land. The angel is human, but not the less an angel for that. The child is divine, but not the less a child for that. At the Caridad, or alms-house, is another of Murillo's great pictures called " Moses Striking the Rock." The majesty with which the great leader of Israel stands before the complaining host is grand.

There is a gallery of paintings at Seville called the Museo. It has but few pictures, and Murillo is the presiding genius of the place. About twenty of his pictures hang here, besides many by Zurbaran and Alonzo Cano. The majority of Murillo's pictures are Conceptions, and he is called by the Spaniards the Conception painter. The faces of his saints and virgins are the same in nearly all his pictures, yet so great is the variety of color, drapery and grouping, that every picture has a charm of its own.

Murillo has not the strength of Michael Angelo, or the naturalness of Velazquez. He has not that ideality of Raphael which can bring the heavenly to earth; but he has that power which can exalt the earthly to heaven, which can rid humanity of all that is sensual and earthly, and clothe it with all the grace of spiritual beauty. Looking at the face of Murillo, you would not think him a man of tender sentiment. Yet his life, work, and all his subjects show it. One circumstance will show the sentiment of the man. There now hangs in the Sacristy in the cathedral a celebrated picture, a Descent from the Cross, by Campana, a pupil of Michael Angelo. So life-like is it that one great artist, Pachecho, said that he was afraid to remain with it after dark. This picture once hung in the parish church of Murillo, called Santa Cruz. It was with him a great favorite. He used to stand before it watching, as he said, until those holy men had finished the taking down of the sacred body of Jesus. Before this picture he wished to be buried, and his wish was gratified. A plain marble slab in the church of Santa Cruz marked the spot where he was laid under this picture, with this inscription: "*Vive Moriturus.*" Marshal Soult, the vandal who robbed Spain of its treasures, destroyed this church, scattered the bones of Murillo, and tore this grand picture into five pieces. It has now been restored and hangs in the cathedral. This picture is not equal to Rubens' Descent from the Cross. Two men in Jewish dress, on ladders, are letting down the lifeless form with its drooping head, the body pale and bathed in blood, while the Virgin mother, Mary Magdalen, and the other women, are gathered around the foot of the cross, with their sorrowful faces turned up to the lifeless body.

It is here at Seville that Murillo can be seen, or rather felt, in all his glory. He was a true Andalusian, fond of beauty and ravishing color, proud and high-tempered. Of all the bright stars in the galaxy of Spanish artists, he is the brightest.

THE OLIVE AND THE VINE.

We can reach Cadiz from Seville by railway, and by the boat down the Guadalquivir. The distance is about one hundred miles. The valley of the Guadalquivir is one of the most fertile parts of Spain. Its olives, olive oil, wine, oranges and cork are noted, and form staple articles of commerce. An olive farm, or Hacienda, as it is called, is worthy of a visit, and we pass by many of them on our way to Cadiz. It is at once a country home of the owner, a village for his laborers, and a manufactory where men, women and children work alike. A good Hacienda will contain 20,000 trees planted in rows. The trees have a beautiful green color, but no other beauty. They resemble our large water willows. Each tree produces from two to three bushels of olives, the value of which is about one dollar. The olive is planted in January. A branch is cut from the parent stock, four slits made in the largest end, and a stone put between them and inserted in the ground and a bank made around it. It is watered for two years, but yields little return till the tenth year, and is in its prime at its 30th year. The finest trees are produced by grafting upon the wild olive. The berries, when ripe, are of a dark purple color. In the autumn, when the gathering commences, the orchards are a lively scene. The men, clothed in sheep-skins, mount the trees and whip off the fruit with sticks; the children pick them up, and the women drive the donkeys laden with them to the mill. The fruit is ground into a pulp between two mill-stones turned by mules. The mass is then put into round mats or baskets, about the size and shape of a large cheese, and these are piled one upon another under a large press, and the oil extracted, which runs into a large vat below, partly filled with water. The impurities sink into the water, and the oil rises to the top and is dipped off into earthen jars, which are sunk in the earth, and which hold about 1,000 gallons each, and here it is allowed to clarify and settle. The refuse from the press is used for fuel and to fatten pigs. The olive berry, when used for eating, is picked just before it is ripe, to preserve its green color. The oil of Spain is not so pure and delicate as that of Lucca. The first quality is used as food, but the second grade is thick and green, and is exported for making soap.

The railway passes through Jerez, from whence comes our Sherry wine. The wine-cellars here are immense establishments, having the appearance of large sheds, each covering acres of ground. They are called Bodegas. Many of them contain 15,000 butts, each holding over one hundred gallons. The stranger is conducted through these immense establishments, and invited to taste all the different kinds of wine, from the crude juice of the grape to the ripe golden sherry. They have great names for the different butts, such as the "Twelve Apostles," "Mathuselah," which is ninety-five years old; "The wine of Jesus Christ," etc. The wines obtained from such well-known houses as R. Davis, Duff Gordon,

M. Pemartin, M. Misa, and P. Garvey, are pure. No good sherry can be bought in Jerez for less than from two and a half to three dollars per gallon, and from that upward for the older wines. Add to this a duty of fifty or sixty per cent., and we may see what is the first cost of a pure sherry wine in this country. Wine of a certain grade—say Amontillado—is cured in a certain butt of immense size. In the bottom of the butt will be found a substance called "mother," similar to that found in barrels of vinegar. Wine is drawn from this butt from time to time, and it is filled as often from more crude wine, and thus the same grade is kept up year after year from the mother or coagulated mass in the bottom.

The Spaniards do not drink the sherry wines, because they are too dear and too strong for their taste. It is far more common in England and America, upon the tables of the rich, than in Spain. Even in Seville and Granada, it is rather used as a delicate liqueur than as a common beverage. The only time we saw any sherry in Spain was at the house of the foreign Ministers, and at the reception of Mr. Canovas, the President of the Cabinet. It is made *by* foreigners and *for* foreigners. The sherry, although a pure wine, is the result of a mixture of many different kinds of wines of a great variety of flavor ; and the process of tasting, mixing, correcting, adding and subtracting from the different butts, until the required color, body, flavor, aroma and dryness is obtained, is the work of years. The taster, who is called the Capataz, thus becomes the most important man of the Bodega, and the autocrat of the business. He is ordinarily a mountaineer from the Asturian mountains, who spends his life in sipping wines. Fine old sherry is of a rich brown color, and the newer wines are paler. The quantity of alcohol in the natural sherry is about twenty per cent. And even in addition to this, to prepare it for shipping, brandy must be added. There are sweet wines of the sherry grape with all the flavor of sherry wine. It has the delicacy and the deliciousness of Johannisberger.

It will be seen that no really pure and good sherry can be had in this country for less than five dollars a gallon. Price may be one test of the purity of a wine; but, considering the vast amount of wine which is manufactured and doctored in this country and France, the only guaranty for a good wine is the house from which it is purchased. But the truth requires us to say that much, and perhaps most, of the so-called wine sold in America is a manufactured compound destructive to health. The ordinary drink of the better classes in Spain is the common red wine, generally the Valdepenas. It is furnished gratis by all the hotels at the *table d'hôte,* and can be bought at from twenty-five to thirty-five cents per gallon. We saw scarcely an intoxicated person in Spain. Yet here the common people who can afford it are fond of stronger drink than their wine. There is a preparation of anise seed, and also Holland Schnapps, sold in the saloons in small glasses, half as large as a small wine-glass, for a cent a glass.

The great wine merchants of Jerez are generally either French or Scotch. They are wealthy, and live in the suburbs of the city like princes. The olive and the vine are the sources of wealth in Spain. The annual production of wine is about one hundred and thirty-six millions of gallons.

CADIZ.

Two and a half miles from Jerez, on the banks of the Guadelete, is the most famous battle-field of Spain. Here, in 711, was fought for two days the great battle between the Moors under Taric and the Goths under Roderick, which resulted in the entire subversion of the Gothic power and the subjugation of Spain to the Moors. Little by little, and as the result of dissensions among themselves, the Moors lost their conquests, until at length, in 1492, at Granada, Boabdil surrendered the last of their possessions in Spain. The railway which brings us from Seville, passing near this battle-field, brings us to Cadiz, which is situated on the extremity of a long, narrow, semi-circular promontory, extending into the Atlantic ocean very much as Cape Cod does. On the marshes, as we approach, within a few miles of the city, we see numerous heaps of salt, looking like soldiers' tents, white and glistening in the sun. It is made by evaporation in shallow pans from sea water by the heat of the sun. When gathered into a heap shaped like a tent, a fire of brush is built over it until an exterior coating, smooth, glistening, and impervious to rain, is made by the melting of the salt. Here it will stand for years until sold for export.

The promontory on which the city of Cadiz is built is about eight miles long. The peninsula, at the extremity of which the city is built, is a series of rocky ledges from ten to fifty feet high, extending about eight miles from the mainland in a north-westerly direction. On the western side it takes the whole unobstructed force of the Atlantic, and affords on the eastern side a shelter to a splendid inner bay, as large as the bay of New York. So high are the tides and so great the force of the Atlantic, that a massive wall, fifty feet high, is built to protect the city for four miles on the seaward side. On the extreme end of this promontory, which is about three-fourths of a mile wide, Cadiz is built. It has been a famous city from the earliest antiquity. It was founded by Hercules, so the annals say, three hundred years before the days of Romulus and Remus, and was the great and the only port of the Phœnicians and the Romans on the Atlantic. It therefore monopolized all the commerce with England and the Baltic, and became immensely rich. It has always been, and is now, a city of merchants, and therefore its people have not been held in the highest estimation by the Spanish grandees, who, glorying in their descent from renowned cavaliers, even in their poverty affect to despise trade. Although one of the oldest, Cadiz has the air of one of the newest cities of Spain. Ascend the Torre de la Vigia, on which is situated the marine observatory, and you have the whole city at your feet. Every house is whitewashed within and without. Every roof is flat, covered with brick, and cemented so as to catch the rain, on which alone the city depends for water. All is white, and cleanly, and smokeless as if just painted. Numerous elegant little towers rise on the roofs, from which the merchants could watch their galleons coming into the harbor. The narrow peninsula below you is thickly studded with houses, but looks as if the stormy Atlantic, forever battering against its walls, would sweep it out of existence. To the west stretches the trackless ocean, with no land between us and the shores of Virginia. To the east lies the great inner bay, ten miles in width, on the eastern side of which is Puerto Real, the great naval station of Spain, and which once was the rendezvous of the galleys of Cæsar. There is no business in Cadiz except such as is thrust upon it by its harbor. It has lost much of its prestige as a commercial city, and Seville has taken it. Oil, wine, olives, oranges and salt are shipped here in large quantities, but foreigners monopolize much of this business. Before the late wars, Cadiz was a rich city. Their wealth was mostly invested in their own government funds, on which no interest is paid; taxes are high, and the expense of living very great; almost nothing is raised in this part of Andalusia. Bad tillage and want of rain leaves the country barren of almost everything but wheat. Very few vegetables are obtained. The poor live on fish, bread and olives. Meat, chickens and eggs are brought from Tangiers in Morocco. Both poor and rich are obliged to live with the greatest economy. But a Spaniard can live comfortably on almost nothing. The curse of the people is their ignorance. A consular agent informed me that the best people could scarcely write their names, and that many men high in office could not write intelligibly. Another curse, says my guide, is the priests. There are sixty connected with one of the cathedrals here, where three would be enough. The city, being surrounded by water, is resorted to for its cool breezes in the summer, and has therefore become a watering-place.

In the evening, after the terrible heat of the day, the inhabitants come out of their houses and fill the alamedas or squares which face the sea, where they enjoy the cool sea breeze, and spend half the night promenading under the trees and along the shore. Cadiz is noted for its beautiful women, and, says a good authority, "they fascinate alike by their form and their manners. They are more the devotees of Venus than of the chaste Diana."

There are few works of art here worth the traveler's attention. Cadiz has two cathedrals. Even the best is a bad specimen of the overloaded, florid Corinthian style of the last century. But one work of art here we cannot pass by. It is the last picture of Murillo, the "Marriage of St. Catherine," over the high altar in the chapel of the Convent of the Capuchins. When the picture was nearly completed he fell from the scaffold and received injuries from which he died shortly after at Seville. This picture is nine feet by twelve, and has ten figures in it. St. Catherine is kneeling before the Virgin, who holds her son on her knees. He is putting the ring on the finger of the saint, angels standing on each side, and cherubs are hovering above and below. The coloring and the grouping are fine. The priest in attendance told me Murillo was occupied twenty days in painting the picture, which is substantially finished. Here in this convent is also a St. Francis. The saint is kneeling, looking up, enraptured by the heavenly vision of the Saviour dimly seen in the clouds above. His hands are stretched upward, bearing the bloody marks of the nails. They stand out from the canvas like the arms of a living man. The upturned face of holy submission, reverent love, seems an inspiration. Had Murillo never done anything else, this picture would have made him immortal. I asked the ancient friar who attended us, "What did your brethren pay Murillo for this picture?" He said seventy-five dollars.

CADIZ TO GIBRALTAR.

It is possible to go from Cadiz to Gibraltar by diligence in fifteen hours, but it is easier to go by water if the weather is fair. With a splendid waterfront, with the finest harbor in Spain, and one of the finest in the world, Cadiz has only one little wooden dock for small boats, and no dock from which a little steamer can start. It has every commercial advantage—a good harbor, good approach to it, a good country at the back of it, a good railroad to it, and good access to France, England and the United States. It should be a great city, full of enterprise and wealth. But it is dead. No large commercial houses, no manufactories, no business but such as necessarily comes to a port. Our little boat steams out of this magnificent harbor to the northwest, to get around the ledge of rocks about six miles from the city, called the "Sows." This ledge saved the city from destruction when Lisbon was destroyed by an earthquake in 1755. The great tidal wave struck this ledge of rocks and was broken; otherwise it would have rolled over the city and destroyed it.

The view of the city from the ocean is very grand.

It sits like a queen of the sea, white and glistening, surrounded by water, the lofty lighthouse standing like a brilliant gem in her diadem. The lighthouse rises high out of and above a large fort built upon a lofty rock, standing in the sea in advance of the city. Cadiz seen from the south-west, as we turn toward Gibraltar, and looking on her massive sea-girt wall, presents the appearance of one grand fortification, crowned by the cathedral with its lofty tower, which is seen rising far above all. That part of Andalusia along which we are now sailing is full of interest, and its history is older than that of Rome. It was called Tartesus.

The shores of Spain, from Cadiz to the Straits, are a series of high, barren bluffs and long sand points extending into the ocean. Here and there a windmill or an ancient watch-tower is seen on the highest points on the shore, while far inland rise the snow-clad mountains of Andalusia, with occasionally a white village seen nestling among the valleys. In two or three hours we come in sight of a long, low point stretching into the sea, with a lighthouse on its extremity. This is Trafalgar, off which the great battle between Nelson and the combined forces of the French and Spanish was fought, Oct. 21, 1805, which has given England ever since the supremacy of the seas. We pass over the very spot where Nelson lost his life. It is a place which might well inspire the great hero. The enemy were before him in magnificent array. From the deck of his ship he could look through the gates of the Atlantic and the Mediterranean. The headlands of Europe and Africa, rising on either hand, were before him. Here he raised his famous signal, "England expects every man to do his duty." It is said that before one of his other battles he said, "Westminster Abbey or victory!" Strange that after such a victory, purchased by such a death, the English nation should not have laid him in Westminster Abbey. His remains sleep in St. Paul's, where the Iron Duke has also been laid to rest beside him. Passing Trafalgar, we now enter the Straits of Gibraltar, which may be said to commence on the African side with Cape Spartel, and on the European side with Trafalgar. They are here about thirty miles wide, and they grow narrower, until at Tariffa, in Spain, they are only ten miles in width. A current sets through them of about two and a half miles per hour. The water changes immediately as we come within the influence of the current from green to a blue black. The line of color is distinctly marked, and can be seen for miles. The change of color is produced probably by passing from shallow to deep water.

The Atlas chain of mountains in Africa now rise before us in one confused mass of lofty peaks, extending from the coast far inland. Opposite Tariffa we are in the narrowest part of the Straits. Here, on a ledge of rocks entending far into the Straits, is a large fortification and a lighthouse. This fort commands the Straits more than Gibraltar does, as the Straits opposite Gibraltar are twenty miles wide. But it is much more easily assailed than Gibraltar, and not so easily defended. Here rises a magnificent lighthouse, 135 feet high, which can be seen forty miles away. Tariffa in former times has been a place of great importance and the scene of many a gallant contest between the Moors and Christians. Here the Moors first landed in 711, and the first chief who landed, Tarif Malik, gave a name to the town, and here the Moors levied contributions on every passing ship, and hence our English word tariff.

The sail from here through the Straits is a magnificent one. The channel begins to widen into deep bays, between long headlands on either side. The white towers of Tangiers rise at the south. Ships of every description are hurrying through the great highway before a fair wind, with all their canvas spread. To the south-east arises the high, rocky front of Abyle, the African Pillar of Hercules. Soon around another long point, far to the northeast, we descry just the low south point of the rock Gibraltar. As we round the point more and more the view extends, and we see farther and farther up, until we catch a glimpse of Calpe, the European Pillar of Hercules, and soon the whole magnificent rock stands before us, the most impregnable fortress of the world, the object of a hundred battles during a thousand years gone by.

GIBRALTAR AND CONSTANTINOPLE.

There are two places of supreme importance in the present history of the world—Gibraltar and Constantinople. One controls all the commerce between America, Eastern Europe, and all the nations which group themselves around the Mediterranean. The other is the key to all the commerce between the Black Sea, its tributaries, the country drained by the Danube and the Mediterranean, and the outside world. Besides this, Constantinople, standing at the only point where the Continents of Europe and of Asia meet, in these days of railroads and telegraphs, is to be the point at which will converge, and from whence will radiate, all the overland traffic between these two continents. England laid her hand on Gibraltar 174 years ago, and has held it ever since. She took it by force when fighting for Spain, and refused to hand it over to the rightful owner when the war of the Succession was finished. By force she has held it ever since.

By all rules of international law, and by all considerations of equity, it belongs to Spain. It is a part of her territory; it is a constant threat and humiliation to her. But with England, as in the case of Malta, Cyprus and India, might makes right. We are not disposed to quarrel with this principle, which, whether we recognize it in our Code of International Law or not, is a principle acted on by all the enlightened nations of the world.

Put the opportunity in the way of any great nation to aggrandize or protect itself at the expense of a weaker, and what nation does not find a good excuse for so doing in law and in morals? But if England can hold Gibraltar and Malta, why should not Russia hold Constantinople, if she can take it? Why is not might right, here also as well as at Gibraltar? The Russian says, "Why should we, one of the great powers, and even *the* greatest power in Europe, with 90 millions of people, with one-seventh of the territory of the world, be shut out from the Mediterranean? Why should our progress and expanding energies be cramped and shut in, because of the envy of the English nation? If England can hold Gibraltar by force, why cannot we hold Constantinople?" There is no principle of law or justice on which England has acted for the past one hundred years, which would prevent Russia from holding Constantinople if she can get it.

The occupation of Gibraltar by the English has been a constant source of complaint by Spain for a whole century. Not only is it humiliating to her to have a foreign fortress on her soil, with its guns turned upon her dominions, but its occupation is a constant source of trouble from the smuggling of goods from Gibraltar into Spain. Mr. Bright acknowledged to me that England has no right to Gibraltar, and only holds it by the law of force, and at an immense expense, and that he would be willing to cede it to them again. I asked if he would be willing to turn it over with all its formidable fortifications and guns, and with its present strength for doing evil to the commerce of the world? He said no; that he would dismantle it and, by treaty, have it stripped of its ability to threaten the commerce of other nations. He said Mr. Cobden once told him, after he had been traveling in Spain, that if the English would cede Gibraltar to Spain, they could obtain a treaty from Spain in relation to duties and commerce which would be worth millions of pounds annually to England. Now it costs England $1,200,000 dollars annually. We do not wonder, however, that Englishmen hold on to this as one of the jewels in the "crown of the Ocean Queen." It accommodates from 6,000 to 8,000 troops, who, after staying here for one year, are acclimated and prepared for the hotter climate of India. It is one of the chain of fortresses on her grand highway to India; Malta, Cyprus, Aden and Bombay being the others. This is the first great coaling depot on the line from England to the East, and these depots for coal are absolutely necessary for a steam marine; for no war vessel, at its highest efficiency, can carry more than six or eight days' supply of coal. England thus maintains this line of fortifications from her own shores to India, so that her steam marine is irresistible by any other power, and she is literally the mistress of the Mediterranean. She, at Gibraltar, holds the key of this great sea, and controls its commerce. It is true that the Straits are twenty miles wide at Gibraltar, and none of its 80-ton guns can reach the opposite shore, yet they have only to station across the channel a few of their ironclads, supported by the harbor and fortress of Gibraltar, and they completely dominate it. If England could always be at peace with all the world, she is the very best power to hold Gibraltar. But suppose she was at war with America—not one of our ships could safely pass the straits.

It is too late for the nations of the world to complain of the occupation of Gibraltar and Malta. The right has become prescriptive; but what we do contend for is that England cannot, with any consistency, object to other nations occupying strongholds on the map of the world which do not belong to her.

England has not a foot of land on the Continent

of Europe excepting Gibraltar, and probably never will have; but every Englishman who sails into the harbor of Gibraltar, and from the deck of his ship looks up the sloping sides of this rock, three miles long, feels and knows that it is worth more than any whole kingdom on the Continent. He sees, at a glance, that the power which holds this holds the Mediterranean. He sees how impregnable it is, and that all the navies of the world could not take it. He sees the line of granite wall, stretching along the water from the perpendicular eastern face all around the western side and to the northern face, surmounted by eighty-ton guns, pointing in every direction. All along up the slope of the rock, wherever a battery can be placed, there he sees these black, one-eyed monsters looking down upon him. From the deck of the ship in the bay is the best place to get a good view of this fortress. The town consists of two parts, both situate on the western side, near the water. The residence for civilians and for business is on the northerly end of the western side. Then comes the parade ground; then a beautiful park, called the Alameda, with walks, miniature lakes, bridges, rustic seats, and trees and flowers of all kinds; and then on the south-westerly side are situated the houses of the officers and garrisons for the soldiers.

The town of Gibraltar—that is, the civilians' quarters—is built on the slope which rises quite suddenly from the western side of the Rock. Street rises above street for hundreds of feet, and in the evening, when the houses are lighted, it has much the appearance of the old town of Edinburgh viewed from the lower town. It has a population of about eighteen thousand, composed of all races under the sun, and clothed in every garb known to mankind. The largest portion of the people are Roman Catholics. Then the Jews come next in numbers; they have four synagogues. The Protestants are next in number, and then Mohammedans. The inhabitants are traders, and smuggling seems to be the chief part of their business. Thousands of pounds of tobacco, beside immense quantities of other goods, are smuggled into Spain from Gibraltar annually; and when it is remembered that one of the chief sources of revenue to Spain is tobacco, it may be seen what a thorn in the side of Spain is this English fortress. These goods are carried off from Gibraltar in small boats at night to the coast of Spain, where the contrabandista are ready to receive them and carry them into the mountains, and thence to all parts of the kingdom.

The climate here, except from July to October, is salubrious and tempered by the sea breezes; but during the summer months, when the Levanter prevails, it is unhealthy; wounds will not heal then, and diseases prevail among children. During these months the people resort to Africa, along the shores of the Atlantic, west of the Straits, where they get the Atlantic breezes and the climate is salubrious even in summer. There are no springs on the Rock. Immense reservoirs are built on different parts above the town, for storing the water which falls in rain. Their capacity is about twelve thousand tons. There are good hotels here, kept by Englishmen, and everything is done and served in the English style. Every one you meet at the hotels is English, while in the streets there is a strange mixture of all nationalities. But everything you see and hear shows you the military character and government of the place.

When you land outside of the walls you cannot pass the gates without a permit from a government officer, which is a permission for you to remain in the town for five days, when it is supposed you will obtain a renewal of the permit. The gates are closed at sunset and opened at sunrise, at the signal by the booming of the Rock gun on the northern point. If you are without the walls after sunset, you must stay out all night. If you are out of your house after midnight, you are arrested.

You enter the town through the immense gates of a fortification guarded by soldiers. Barracks, men in uniform or marching in ranks, are seen on every hand. The fife, drum and bugle are heard at all hours. There are eight thousand soldiers stationed here. They are under constant drill, and a grand parade of England's best troops may be seen on the parade ground twice a week, at ten o'clock in the morning. It is a fine sight to stand, a little before this hour, on the parade ground, and to see the different companies, clad in their various uniforms, winding down the numerous paths from all directions toward the parade, their burnished arms glistening in the sun as they march to the music of the bugle and the drum. On the parade ground we saw a company of Moors from Morocco, dressed in the Arab style. By the permission of the English government they are here trained by British tacticians and then sent to Morocco to become officers. They were, physically, the finest-looking company on the parade.

Gibraltar is used by England as a half-way station to India, and particularly as a place for acclimating her troops for that latitude. Soldiers, by remaining here two or three years, are prepared for the more enervating influences of a tropical country. Formerly all fortifications and public works were built by civilians; but latterly all this work is done by artisans who are found among the troops, who, for a little extra pay, are glad to relieve the monotony of a soldier's life by labor of this kind. Gibraltar consumes, but produces absolutely nothing. All the meats, poultry and eggs consumed there are brought from Tangiers in Africa, and all their vegetables are brought from the Spanish towns.

GIBRALTAR.—NATURAL FEATURES.

After passing the Straits the northerly coast bears almost due east for about fifteen miles, when it turns suddenly for about twenty miles in a circular line to the north-west, then to the north, and then to the east. At this point the long, wedge-like promontory of Gibraltar extends from the coast due south five miles into the sea, being about one-half mile wide. The northern end of this strip of land for one and a half miles is a sandy beach and belongs to Spain, and a line of white sentry boxes, filled with guards to prevent smuggling, is stretched across from shore to shore. The next four hundred yards to the south is called "neutral ground," on which there is no erection, and not a tree, bush or rock is to be seen. It is no man's land, and no power has any jurisdiction over it. Next south of the neutral ground commences the English jurisdiction. A line of blue sentry boxes on their side also stretches across the promontory, about one-half mile in distance from shore to shore.

About one-half mile to the south of the northerly limit of the English jurisdiction, rises abruptly out of the dead sea level of sand, 1,400 feet high, the Rock of Gibraltar, which extends south three miles into the Mediterranean. There are three points higher somewhat than the remainder of the Rock: one at the northerly end, one in the middle, and one at the southerly end. The latter is called Europa Point or Calpe, and is the European Pillar of Hercules. It looks down upon and through the Straits into the Atlantic. The central point is used as a lighthouse and signal station. From it all vessels approaching the Straits from the east are seen at the distance of thirty or forty miles, and their arrival is immediately telegraphed to London. The view from this point is sublimity itself. Far to the eastward the blue Mediterranean is covered with white sails, all converging toward the Straits. Twenty miles across the Straits rises the African Pillar of Hercules, and far away to the south-west stretches the Atlas Mountains of Africa, while to the north and west arise, peak after peak, the snow-clad mountains of Andalusia. Looking to the west, immediately at your feet, is the Bay of Algeciras, or the harbor of Gibraltar, the westerly and the northerly sides formed by the circular line of the Straits and the easterly side by the promontory of Gibraltar. This harbor is in width about six miles from the Rock to the westerly shore, but has a wide entrance to the south and is much exposed to the

Levanters and southerly winds. The anchorage is not good on account of a rocky bottom.

The town and fortifications are on the western side of the Rock, which rises by a gradual slope from the water's edge to the very top. The eastern side of the Rock, for its whole length of three miles, is one precipitous, almost perpendicular wall from 1,200 to 1,400 feet high, where Nature has reared her everlasting defences, inaccessible to man. You may look down from these dizzy battlements to the Mediterranean surging and roaring below and find no place where an invading foe can obtain a foothold. Not a gun is placed on this eastern side, for none is needed. The north front also, looking down on the narrow beach which connects with the mainland, is very precipitous and rises almost perpendicularly 1,350 feet. On the highest northern point is placed the Rock gun, which is fired at sunrise and at sunset, and by which the gates of the town are opened and shut. From the town, which is at the foot of the western slope, beautiful roads run in zigzag directions up to the very top of the Rock. The southern extremity, or Calpe, or Europa Point, which looks off toward the Straits, gradually breaks down and extends, like a plowshare, one-half mile into the sea.

Such are some of the natural features of this great fortress.

GIBRALTAR.—ITS DEFENCES.

It needs defence only where it can be attacked. The eastern perpendicular wall, as we have said, needs no defence. Europa, or the southern point, and the western side, can be approached from the sea and the northern side from the land. The defences on the southern, western and northern sides are marvelous. For one hundred and seventy years the English nation has been exhausting its skill to render it impregnable. The first defence is a granite outer wall, extending entirely around the western side of the Rock, along the water line from Europa Point to the cliff on the northern extremity. This wall is eight feet thick and fifteen or twenty feet high. It is a series of bastions and batteries and is pierced with port-holes tier above tier for three miles in extent. From these port-holes and from the glacis on the top of the wall are seen pointing in every possible direction those huge eighty-ton guns which look like an army of black, sleeping fiends.

Europa Point is the most exposed to attack from the water and is most magnificently fortified. Tier above tier of immense walls and fort above fort filled with guns rise on this point for two hundred feet. The north front protects against any approach from the land. Six hundred and fifty feet above the water a gallery one-half mile in length has been tunneled into the Rock across the northern front and near the face of the cliff, and one hundred feet above that is another gallery, and above that another. There are two and a half miles of these galleries along this northern cliff. From them port-holes have been opened to the northern end of the cliff, through which immense guns frown down on Spain and the narrow approach from the land across the neutral ground. These galleries are about twelve feet wide, and the rooms for the guns hollowed out along their course are about twenty feet square. Rooms also, for storing shot, shell, powder and supplies are scattered along these galleries high up in the heart of the Rock. At the eastern extremity of one of these galleries is a large hall excavated, called the Hall of St. George, where Nelson was once entertained. There are batteries also on the ledges outside on this northern cliff, which fairly bristles with these great guns, and, like a huge giant stands scowling ominously down upon Spain from these deep-mouthed port-holes tier above tier. On the exterior northern point is the great Rock gun, which, on the morning of the Queen's birthday, booms forth its grand salute; the next battery below takes up the fire, then the next gallery, and so on down and down, until the shore batteries shake the whole Rock by their thunders, when the troops close up the grand salute to the sovereign Queen, who, sitting in her little isle, holds the keys of the world's fortress and sways her sceptre over some of the fairest portions of the globe.

GIBRALTAR IMPREGNABLE.—ITS HISTORY.

Gibraltar is impregnable. With provisions and water for a long siege, manned by 10,000 men, all the navies of the world combined could make no impression on her walls. And no army, however numerous, could approach it across the narrow sandy strip of neutral ground which connects it with the mainland. This approach can be submerged, and a thousand guns from the galleries along the northern face frown down upon it.

We had a rare opportunity of seeing in operation the defensive qualities of this great fortress. Lord Napier had just been appointed commander of the fortress. It is customary for every new commander to visit all the batteries and to see all the guns along the shore batteries fired. We were standing on the top of the central rock at the signal station when this grand display opened. The commander, with his staff, commenced with the southern batteries on the shore, and passed on northward from one to another along a line of two and a half miles. First we would see the fire belching forth; then clouds of smoke rising and rolling up the sides of the rock; then slowly broke upon the ear the thunder of the huge guns, which shook the mountain to its foundations and re-echoed back from the rock until it was lost far away amid the mountains of Spain and Africa. About twenty artillerymen manned each gun. At a certain word of command they put in a cartridge; at another they rammed it home; at another they ran the gun out of the port-hole; at another elevated or lowered her muzzle, as the lieutenant sighted her; at another they pulled the lanyard which fires the cap.

It was a magnificent sight, and those eighty-ton guns, belching forth fire and smoke, and shaking the rock by their thunder, gave a vivid idea of what the terrible reality would be were the thousands of these black monsters, bristling all over the great fortress, turned on some devoted enemy. Except by treachery or starvation, Gibraltar never can be taken.

Its history for two thousand years past has been a romance. It has been associated with the great struggles between Paganism and Christianity, and between Christianity and Mohammedanism. The Phœnicians, as long ago as the time of Jonah, knew the Straits. They called the Rock Kalpe. It seems never to have been occupied as a fortress until the Moors, under the fiery Tarik, took it in 711. He called it after his own name, Gebal Tarik, or the Hill of Tarik, which name, through the transmutation of language, has become Gibraltar. An old castle is still standing about half-way up the rock, which was built by the Moors in the eighth century.

Gibraltar was taken from the Moors in 1309 by Spain, since which the arms of the city have been a castle with a gate, and a key hanging from it, signifying that this was the key of the Straits, as it has ever since been. In 1333 the Moors again took the fortress, and held it till 1462. The English and Dutch forces took it in the war of the succession, while fighting in the cause of Archduke Charles in 1704, and although at first they considered it a "barren rock" and a "useless charge," the English have ever since held it. It was besieged in 1779 by the allied powers of France and Spain, and the siege lasted four years. It was conducted with all the skill and with all the accessories then known to the assailants. But on the famous 13th of September, 1783, their formidable floating batteries were destroyed by the English under "Old Elliott." He saved the jewel to the English crown, and here he died, and here he was buried, and his monument now stands ever overlooking the scene of his heroic defence.

Gibraltar is an English Colony; the law of England is administered in Gibraltar. The Judge Advocate has cognizance of all cases in civil matters, and an appeal lies from his decision to the Privy Council in England in all cases involving over £300.

There is a large police force, under a police magistrate, who is charged with keeping the peace among civilians; but the military code is administered in the garrison.

TANGIER.

About thirty miles distant from Gibraltar, diagonally across the Straits, lies Tangier, the seaport of Morocco, situated at the head of a long open bay. Gibraltar could hardly exist without Tangier. It obtains from thence all its beef, chickens and eggs. The Rock of Gibraltar is absolutely barren. Not a vegetable or a spire of grass grows there. Two or three times a week a steamer plies between Gibraltar and Tangier for traffic. Here reside the Consuls and Ministers to Morocco. The city is built of white stone, on a hill sloping backward from the shore to a lofty eminence, crowned with a castle, the residence of the Governor, and containing the prison, filled with the most disgusting specimens of humanity in filth and rags, all huddled together in one room. There were fifty or more of the most desperate-looking men, some with chains on their legs. Here they are allowed to starve, unless their friends help them, for they receive nothing but a little bread and water.

The will of the Emperor, as he is called, is the law, and all crimes are punished according to the whim of the pasha who governs the province. But summary punishment produces a good effect, and crimes are of rare occurrence. The captain of the steamer told me he often brought from Tangier to Gibraltar fifty thousand silver dollars at a time, and that he had never lost one, and that droves of cattle are constantly coming from the interior, and not one was ever stolen. The punishment for petty theft is to be put naked on a donkey and driven through the streets by soldiers, who lash the back of the victim until it streams with blood, while he is obliged to proclaim aloud his crimes. If a robbery is committed on travelers in any district, the Government levies on the district twice the amount stolen, and the Sheik is obliged to collect it. Any traveler into the rural districts is furnished by his Consul with a Government soldier as guard. The soldier is responsible with his life for the return of his traveler.

Tangier has about 12,000 inhabitants, about one-half of whom are Jews and the remainder Mohammedans from all Arabic-speaking countries. The ancestors of the Jews fled from Spain when banished by Charles V. There are no fine buildings in the city. It has two mosques of small dimensions, but so sacred that no Christian is allowed to set foot in them. The most striking objects in Tangier are the Moorish men and Jewish women. There are no finer specimens of humanity than some of the Moors we saw here. They were six and a half feet tall, of fine proportions, dignified carriage, high forehead, black beard, large, soft black eyes, with a natural dignity and grace, and a walk like a king. When dressed, with a fine robe of white hanging gracefully over his shoulders, with a white turban, bound with red or green, and everything about him scrupulously clean, he is a picture of all that is grand in the human frame. We could understand the love of Desdemona for the Moor of Venice. These are the true descendants of the Berber race which conquered Spain, and who, single-handed, were always more than a match for the bravest and proudest knights of Spain in the days of Ferdinand and Isabella. It is said that the Queen refused to allow her knights to accept the challenges of the Moors to single combat, for the Moors were found to be the best warriors.

The Moors who fled from Granada came to this part of Africa. They brought with them their title deeds to the lands held by them in Spain, and their descendants now in Tangier and Tetuan still, after the lapse of four centuries, hold these deeds against the day when they shall return across the Straits and be restored to their former possessions, which they firmly believe is to be their destiny.

Moorish women are never seen in the streets, but I am told by ladies who reside here that they are finer looking than the men. Jewish women are seen in the street, and we can testify to their great beauty. They have fine eyes, rich brunette complexion, a graceful walk, and are well proportioned and always well dressed. A Moorish wedding is the thing to see in Tangier. The bridegroom pays for his bride to her father $40 and upward, according to the means and station of the parties. The marriage is a civil contract entered into, written out, and signed before a notary. On the night of the wedding, after the marriage, the bride is carried in a covered chair through the streets, with music and fireworks, to the house of the groom. There is a general entertainment for men in one room and women in another, at the house of the bride's father, on the eve of the wedding, where tea, coffee and sweets are given. The ladies are allowed to see the bride dressed, and I was told by some English ladies at the British Consulate that the dress of the bride in high life was magnificent. All the dowry of the bride goes for this, as it sometimes does in other enlightened countries. The wedding is witnessed only by the parents of the bride and bridegroom. The ceremony is at the house of the bride's father, and never at the mosque, for the women go to the mosque only once a year. The bridegroom sees his bride for the first time on the night of the wedding, when he takes her to his own home. I asked my guide, a splendid-looking Moor: "Suppose he does not like his wife when he sees her, what then?" Said he, "Then he can get another."

Another thing to see in Tangier is the market on market day. It is held just outside the walls, on the landward side, in a large square, where almost every imaginable thing is for sale by men in every imaginable garb. Camels from Fez file in with their loads; donkeys from the country with eggs, chickens and vegetables. There are oranges by the million, grain, salt, and dry goods. All these things are scattered about in heaps, and beside them squat groups of Arabs, each with a loose-flowing garment, like a cloak, with a hood thrown over the head; while walking about you see the aristrocratic Moor, with his large turban, white, flowing dress and yellow slippers; the rich Jew in his broadcloth mantle and silk vest; the black merchant from Timbuctoo, and the dark African, with his face scarred by his captors—all meet here in one strange medley, seen nowhere else except in Mohammedan cities.

Tangier ought to be and will be a great city. It is situate in the midst of the Straits, where passes the commerce of all nations, and where the commerce of North-eastern Africa, even to the interior deserts, centres, and it has a good climate. Here those seeking health may come, and here the artist may find a Moorish city full of quaint subjects for his pencil and a country around full of all natural grandeur.

MOROCCO.

The northern coast of Africa was once one of the strongholds of the false prophets, and from thence they threatened the liberty of Europe. They first broke up into independent powers, and now these have nearly run their race. Morocco is now a kingdom of about 230,000 square miles, or one-sixth larger than France. It extends along the Atlantic from the Straits southward from 700 to 800 miles, and along the Mediterranean from the Straits about 250 miles, and south from the Mediterranean about 500 miles, and reaches into the Desert. It is composed of mountainous ranges, which run north-east from the Atlantic to the Mediterranean, with fertile intervening valleys, which are well watered by rivers which flow from the water-shed into the Atlantic and the Mediterranean on one side, and into the Desert, where they are swallowed up, on the other. One of these rivers—the Muluya—is 400 miles long, and is the boundary between Morocco and Algeria.

Fez, which is about 75 or 100 miles south of the Straits is the capital where the Emperor—or the Sultan, as he is also called—resides. It is in a wide, fertile valley, between parallel chains of mountains. Between these mountains the climate is delightful, scarcely ever falling below 40 degrees or rising above 90. The slopes of the mountains looking down on the Straits and facing the Atlantic are beautifully wooded and afford delightful winter residences for invalids from Europe and America, and summer residences for the inhabitants of Gibraltar and the southern coast of Spain. The mountains shield them from the hot winds of the Desert, and the cool breezes of the Atlantic preserve a salubrious temperature. There is a wide range of products, among which are wheat, barley, maize, rice, sugar-cane, figs, pomegranates, lemons, oranges, dates, cotton, tobacco and hemp.

It is easy to see that such a country, with such a climate and such a variety of products, is destined to sustain a large and civilized population, and in the near future it will be one of the most important parts of Africa. It would not surprise us to awake some morning and find that it had been annexed to England. They would then control both ends and the middle of the Mediterranean. Two-thirds of the entire trade of Morocco is now in the hands of British merchants. Caravans of camels from Soudan and Southern Morocco may be seen filing into Tangier—the only port of Morocco—loaded with drugs, red, yellow and green leather, wool, hides, cotton and tobacco; and they bear back cotton, linen and muslin goods, sugar and tea, even as far as Timbuctoo, all of which comes from England. Immense amounts of beef, eggs and poultry are taken to Gibraltar. The captain of the Gibraltar steamer told me that some days he carried across the Straits 500,000 eggs, which cost in Tangier 80 cents per 100, and oranges, we found, were 25 cents per 100. Beef was sold for $7 per 100 pounds. One hundred head of cattle were taken to Gibraltar on the steamer with us. They were brought alongside in a scow. A noose was put round their horns, which by a rope was fastened to a steam windlass on board the steamer. In one-half minute the animal is raised by his horns into the air before he has time to struggle, and swung round over the steamer and then let down into the hold.

The Sultan is supposed to be the owner of the soil, and it is rented, as in Egypt, to tenants at a very low rate, and the land descends to the heir of the tenant, subject to the rental. The taxes are very light, but the revenue is raised chiefly from export and import duty. The Sultan owes a national debt, incurred in the war with Spain, but he pays his interest, and in this respect his government does not suffer in comparison with that of many of our States. As he is an arbitrary prince, and his word is the law of the land, he has only to impose a tax on one or more of the twenty-nine districts and the governor must collect it.

Not only are there beautiful winter residences along the wooded slopes of the Straits, but the means of living are abundant and cheap, and the sports are excellent. There are here plenty of partridge, hare and rabbits, but the great sport is the boar hunt. We saw on Sunday morning a company of about twenty ladies and gentlemen, English and French, on horseback, leaving Tangier for the hills about ten miles distant. The hunters are allowed no weapon but a spear. From fifty to one hundred men are employed to beat up the bush and drive the animals out into the open, when the sport commences by running down the boar. When he turns at bay he is an ugly customer, but the poor dogs and horses generally bear the brunt of the fight.

MALAGA.

THE traveler should either approach or leave Gibraltar by water. From the harbor and the Straits only can you see the mighty proportions of this fortress at one glance, and see how grandly isolated it stands, dominating the great highway of the nations.

We sailed from Gibraltar in a small steamer for Malaga, a distance of about fifty miles. We pass from the northwest side of the Rock entirely around to the north-east side of it, passing Rock Gun Point on the north, under the line of frowning batteries, rank above rank on the west side, past the signal tower on the highest central point, and bend around Calpe, the southern point from whose tower you can see over the mountains into the harbor of Cadiz seventy miles away to the north-west. From every different point of observation the rock presents an entirely different appearance. Immediately on passing the southern extremity, Europa Point, to the east, the Straits widen to the north, and here commences the Mediterranean.

It is said by geologists that the sea was once

separated from the Atlantic Ocean at the Straits, and that the two continents were here united. As we continue our course eastward the Rock is the one grand object in view, but always receding, until we reach and turn the headlands of Malaga, when it suddenly vanishes from sight. As we turn this long promontory, Malaga bursts upon our view, nestled between the mountains and the sea.

It lies at the eastern extremity of a beautiful vega, 9 miles wide by 18 miles long, bounded by the snow-capped mountains of Granada on the north-east, by the mountains of Ronda on the north, and washed by the waves of the Mediterranean on the south. Its atmosphere is tempered in summer by the snow-clad mountains, and in winter by the sea-breezes from the shores of Africa. It is watered by artificial irrigation from the mountains. Nothing can surpass its fertility and the variety of its productions. The gardens in January were filled with roses and flowers; immense orchards of oranges were on every hand loaded with fruit. The almond, the pomegranate, the palm, the sugar-cane, the grape, the olive, and all kinds of grain were abundant.

As we were obliged to land from the steamer in little boats, we became the prey of boatmen who charged us what they pleased. They held our baggage until their demands were paid, while the policemen looked on as disinterested spectators, without interference, Boatmen, cabmen, and porters have their own way in most cities of Spain.

Malaga has an air of thrift and business unusual for Spain. The streets are made narrow, for the summer climate requires this; but new streets are being opened, and large, fine houses are being erected. There are here manufactories of sugar and two cotton mills which employ 4,000 men, beside manufactories of iron, lead and licorice. The finest raisins are cured here, and certain kinds of wine are made here, such as the sweet muscatel and montilla, which have a wide reputation, but which are too delicate to be exported. The business streets are full of activity, and at night are brilliantly lighted. The cafés are numerous and large, well-lighted and decorated, and in the evening filled with all classes of the people, both rich and poor, high and low, much as if the Bowery boys and Fifth Avenue gentlemen should meet at Delmonico's. There seems to be less social distinction in Spain than in any other country. You will often meet a man clothed in rags ready to receive a gratuity. Yet his dilapidated cloak covers a haughty aristocrat, proud of his high descent, which secures him respect from those appparently above him in social life. In these cafés they sit around small tables, enjoy their sweet drinks with a few cheap cakes, every one talking vociferously, every one smoking, while a band of music adds a sweet element to the confusion. But there is no carousing, and no strong drink or drunkenness. In many of the cafés there are billiard tables, plays, and dances.

Malaga has a large modern cathedral built on the site of the grand mosque of the Moors of which nothing remains but a fine Gothic portal. The cathedral was commenced in 1538 and completed in 1719, and combines some of the bad features of all modern styles of architecture. It has three lofty naves, with heavy massive Corinthian pillars with highly ornamented capitals, but without grace or beauty, and is surmounted by a lofty dome 300 feet high. The population is 110,000; the harbor is small but convenient, and filled with shipping. The hotels are large and airy, usually surrounding a spacious court with a fountain in the centre and filled with flowers. There are beautiful plazas in the city filled with trees and fountains. It has just completed water-works, which bring a great supply of cool, pure water from the mountains nine miles distant. Malaga has a history which reaches back to immemorial antiquity. It was probably founded by the Phœnicians, and became in turn Carthagenian, Roman, Gothic, Moorish and Christian. Ferdinand and Isabella took it from the Moors in 1487, after a dreadful and protracted siege, in which the women and children perished from starvation. Heavy guns called Lombards won the victory for the Christians. The Moors were, through all this struggle, a match for the Christians in the open field, but powder and guns recently brought from Germany won the day. As Napoleon once said, "Providence was on the side which had the heaviest artillery." The wary Ferdinand induced the people to surrender their money, jewels and property as part payment for their freedom, and then gave them eight months in which to raise the balance among their friends. In this way he induced them not to secrete their valuables. After stripping 15,000 people of all they had and setting them to begging among their friends for the remainder of the ransom, he sold them all into perpetual slavery on their failure to pay the full amount. The ancient chronicles, as copied by Irving, describes the wail of these poor people when driven from their homes as heart-rending beyond description. To the stranger, Malaga seems one of the most delightful cities of Spain. The climate is especially adapted to invalids. It has a very dry atmosphere and constant sunlight. It is said that rain falls on only twenty-nine days in the year, and then only for a few hours in each day. Its climate is one of the most equable in Europe. In summer it is open to the breezes from the sea, and resort can be had to any altitude among the mountains. In winter it is sheltered from the winds by mountains at the north and east, so that frost is unknown. The snow-clad mountains are in sight on one side and the blue Mediterranean on the other. Surely this rich and smiling vega of Malaga, with all its beauty and fertility, with its sunlight and sea breezes, its mountains and the Mediterranean, is, as the Moors were accustomed to call it, " Paradise on Earth."

MALAGA TO CORDOVA.

We have only two ways of egress from Malaga, one by water along the coast north-east to Valencia, and the other by railroad northward to Cordova. As we desire to pass out of Spain by way of Valladolid, Burgos and Irun, we take the latter. Our way lies to the north-west up through the vega for about twenty miles. In the suburbs of the city, we pass the large manufactories of wine, sugar and cotton; then the beautiful villas of the rich citizens of Malaga, surrounded by gardens filled with every variety of tropical trees, fruits and flowers. Artificial streams of water for irrigation are flowing on every hand. It is early in January and before seven o'clock in the morning, yet the air is genial and balmy as we rapidly ascend toward the mountains through this beautiful vega. As the sun rose over the lofty hills and threw its light into this valley, it seemed a fairy land too beautiful for this world.

The air was fragrant from the groves of oranges, which extended for miles on every side, loaded with the golden fruit. The roses and the almond trees were in bloom. The sound of flowing waters from the hills was everywhere heard, and the swift streams glistened through the green foliage in every direction. The Moors here brought agriculture to a state of perfection. And here their works for irrigation still continue and carry water to every tree in the whole vega. The mountains, covered with perpetual snow, are the perennial source of these waters during the summer, and no stream is allowed to run its free course to the sea. It is captured far up among the hills, diverted in all directions, divided and subdivided as it descends, going from farm to farm, from garden to garden, from tree to tree, until its poetry and even itself is lost in practical utility. Here the palm and the grape abound and here are produced the famous wines, the Muscatel and Montilla, while the common wine, Valdepenas, furnished free in all hotels in Spain, is here remarkably fine, and can be purchased for thirty or forty cents per gallon. Having passed up this charming valley about twenty miles, we come face to face with the mountains, with no way apparent through them. Suddenly we strike upon and follow the little stream, the Guadalhorce, piercing its way through the wildest gloomy gorges, with perpendicular walls of rock on each side, grand, weird and strange, where the little stream and the railroad contend for the passage. This wonderful gorge—called by the Spaniards the Hoyo or the grave—is equal to the wildest scenery of Switzerland, and almost rivals the royal gorge of the Arkansas in Colorado. With scarcely room for a locomotive to pass, we wind between the rocky wall through miles of tunnels, under the mountain, along by precipices, over bridges and viaducts, until we emerge upon a high plateau 1400 feet above Malaga. Here the whole aspect of nature is changed. Instead of the warm salubrious air of the vega of Malaga, where no frost ever comes, we breathe the crisp, sharp air of the mountains, with frost and ice all around us. We are now on the high plateau of central Spain, and are approaching Teba, a small place where are situated the estates of the ex-Empress Eugenie. Before her marriage she was countess of Teba. From her lofty throne she has descended to again take her place as countess of a little domain far up among the hills of Andalusia; so easily do they make and unmake emperors and empresses, kings and queens, in France and Spain. Here we bid farewell to orange groves, the palm and the vine, and now come upon immense orchards of olives. They cover the whole country, hills, valleys and plains. As far as the eye can reach it is one continuous forest of green, with here and there an immense mill for grinding the fruit standing upon the hills. The distant mountain sides are covered with immense flocks of sheep guarded by shepherds. At Cordova we strike the road which brought us from Madrid, and by this we return to the capital.

MADRID TO BAYONNE.

THE distance from Madrid to the frontier of France is about 400 miles. The journey can be made in twenty hours of continuous traveling. It will take us through Avila, Medina del Campo, Valladolid and Burgos. Each of these places is worthy of a visit. About seventy-five miles from Madrid we reach

AVILA,

a little city of about six thousand inhabitants, set upon a hill with an extended view of plain on one side and mountains on the other. It is beautiful for situation, surrounded by a perfect wall of granite 40 feet high and 12 feet thick, which is surmounted by towers, so that the city was once considered an impregnable fortress.

Its altitude is so great, and its surroundings of vega and mountains so delightful, that it affords a cool and favorite summer resort for the citizens of Madrid. It has a cathedral commenced in the eleventh century, and numerous churches, some of them made famous as the burial places of heroes in Church or State.

Avila is another of the cities which the Spaniards fondly believe was built by Hercules. With the well-known twelve labors he was fated to perform, it would seem that he had sufficient occupation without building most of the cities of Spain. Notwithstanding the Spaniards firmly believe in Hercules as their great master builder, they also believe that he rent a way between Gibraltar and Ceuta for the Mediterranean to flow into the Atlantic, and that he erected his mighty pillars to signalize the event.

Avila is celebrated as the birthplace of two distinguished characters. The first was Alfonso Tostado de Madrigal, who died in 1445, whose doctrines were so luminous, says his biographer, that he made the blind to see, "though Don Quijote declared them more voluminous than luminous." The second was "Our Seraphic Mother, the Holy Theresa, Spouse of Jesus," born here 1515, and who was made lady patroness of Spain by Philip III, and, with the Virgin Mary and St. James, shares the honors of worship in all Spain. She is a favorite subject with the Spanish painters, and her pictures are found in all the galleries of the kingdom. But St. Theresa was not a mere mythical character. She was a real actor, a mystic writer, and reformer of the Carmelite Order. She was translated to heaven, where she received the plans for nunneries of her order, and on her return she carried out those plans in founding numerous convents. One of the doctrines which she taught may be commended to the consideration of the theologians of our day, namely, that the future punishment of the wicked consists in the impossibility of their loving or being loved.

The Spaniards believe that Christ himself conveyed his bride to heaven at her death, while ten thousand martyrs gathered around her dying bed. This makes the second spouse of Christ found in Spain, St. Catherine being the other—too many by one.

Continuing our journey northward for about fifty miles, we pass Medina del Campo, a place of no especial interest, except that here died the good Queen Isabella. At her request her remains were borne by a grand and mournful cavalcade four hundred miles to Granada for burial.

About twenty miles farther north lies the famous ancient capital,

VALLADOLID.

It is a city of fifty thousand inhabitants, but mainly interesting as the scene of great historical events. It was the residence of the Kings of Castile until Philip II made Madrid the capital, in 1560.

Here died Christopher Columbus, on the 20th of May, 1506, at No. 7 Street of Columbus, of a broken heart. His great patroness, Queen Isabella, had died before, and with her died his last hope of justice from the hands of her wary, selfish and politic husband Ferdinand. At Salamanca, about sixty miles southwest of Valladolid, he discussed with the

Augustine monks his theory of the rotundity of the earth. There his arguments were refuted by Scripture, and he was declared an infidel. And now we are standing by the house where he closed his glorious career, cheated in life of rewards solemnly promised to him, and ever since cheated of the honor of giving his name to the continent which he discovered. Even his bones have not been allowed to rest in peace. In 1536 they were borne over the ocean to San Domingo, and from thence in 1795 to Havana.

Here at Valladolid lived Cervantes while he was publishing his "Don Quijote." Here was born Philip II, and here he celebrated his first Auto da Fé, under the auspices of the Inquisition, which destroyed Spain, by putting to death her best citizens, driving out the Jews and Moors, thus banishing all its industry and thrift, and leaving in place thereof haughty superstition and indolence. Well have the Jews and the Moors been avenged. The blood of the Protestants in Holland, of the Aztecs in Mexico, of the Incas in Peru, of the thousands tortured by the Inquisition, has called to heaven for retribution. It has been the most priest-ridden, poverty-stricken, indolent, ignorant, and superstitious nation of Europe. Her most Catholic sovereigns, virgins, and patron saints could not save her. She has for three centuries been paying the penalty of a century of crime. She stands as a warning to all civilized nations.

BURGOS.

AT Valladolid the railroad turns to the north-east, in which direction lies Burgos, distant about 90 miles. On account of its historical associations, its cathedral and other venerable edifices, it possesses great interest.

It was the ancient capital of Castile and Leon, and has been the dwelling-place, and is the burying-place, of many distinguished men of past centuries.

The city lies in the plain of the Arlanzon, which bounds it on one side, while a lofty hill, crowned with an ancient castle, overlooks and dominates it on the other. The ascent to the castle is almost perpendicular for hundreds of feet, and from the top you see the lofty peaks of the Pyrenees at the north. Nearer, the fruitful valley of the Arlanzon spreads like a map before you, while at your feet lies the city, filled with its ancient castles of kings and princes; but the gem of all is the cathedral, which rears its elegant and stately spires immediately beneath your gaze.

Unlike most of the cities of Spain, Burgos has nothing Moorish in its architecture, but it is a fair specimen of the style of the old Gothic Castilian race. Here, after the irruption of the Moors, the scattered remnants of the Goths began to gather their forces, and at last became consolidated into a new kingdom, until, under St. Ferdinand, it became a power capable of coping with the Moors. From this city, as his capital, he carried on his conquests against the infidels, until he wrested Cordova from them in 1235.

In these ages of the Crusades, love of adventure and military renown brought here to the aid of the Christians large numbers of the military religious orders which had their origin in Palestine, such as the Knight Templars, the Knights of St. John, the Teutonic Knights. From the same causes and at this time arose those famous Spanish orders of Alcantara and Santiago, composed of fanatics, half priest and half soldier, of whom Cortez was a fair specimen. One beautiful remnant of the Teutonic order still remains, in the residence of the Captain General, which was once the castle of the order. The property of all the orders has long since been confiscated by the Crown.

The castle, which overlooks the city, once the residence of kings, though now dilapidated, is full of memories of centuries gone by.

Here the Cid was married, and also Edward I, of England, to Eleanor of Castile.

Here the Cid held his King Alphonso VI as captive, till he exacted an oath that he was not concerned in the assassination of his brother. This oath was administered in the church St. Aguida, just at the foot of the castle, not upon the Bible, but upon an iron lock, which is still hanging on the wall, where it has been for 800 years. The fortress was built a thousand years ago, and has stood many sieges since. Here Wellington besieged the French, shut up in this castle for 35 days, but was obliged to retire with great loss.

The cathedral is considered one of the finest in Spain. Inferior buildings crowd upon it, so that it is difficult to get a good view of its exterior, unless we ascend to the castle. There its beautiful proportions and tall, fragile spires stand out in contrast with the mean buildings about it. The west front has two spires of delicate open work, 300 feet high, and on the centre rises a beautiful dome, 200 feet high, surrounded by turrets of open work, all light, graceful and chaste. The rich carving on the doorways and towers reminds you of the church of Notre Dame, of Paris. You enter one of these lofty sculptured doors, with its beautiful Gothic arch. Three naves, 300 feet long and 200 feet high, supported by massive columns, each crowned by a perfect Gothic arch, stretch out before you, a picture of perfect architectural proportions, symmetry and beauty. At the transept the church is 250 feet broad, and here, where it crosses the central nave, rises the magnificent dome, or lantern, which gives light to the coro and the high altar.

The coro is, as usual in Spanish cathedrals, in the centre of the church. It has seats for a choir of over 100, and each seat is most elaborately wrought in mahogany, illustrating Bible characters and scenes; around the sides of the exterior naves are a large number of chapels, many of them tombs of distinguished characters.

These chapels contain some few pictures of merit. One has a crucifix, carved by Nicodemus, which traversed the sea alone, and found a resting place here.

These chapels are well supplied with virgins, decked out in tinselry and finery, looking much like over-grown and over-dressed dolls.

One would suppose if they must have a Virgin to worship that, under the inspiration of such a cathedral, they could mould her face with a little more art and dress her with some degree of taste, and that they would remember that she was a meek and lowly maiden of Judea, of humble life and manners.

How would she have appeared walking the streets of Nazareth or Jerusalem, tricked out with bits of lace, ribbons, gilt breast pin, bracelets and ear-rings. This depraved taste is shown in all Catholic countries where the influence of a Raphael, a Murillo, a Correggio in elevating the taste, has not been able to counteract the debasing influence of this corrupt desire in the uneducated mind for the worship of graven images. Religion, in pandering to this desire, has brought a reproach on itself, has turned to ridicule one of the most unique, pure and lovely characters of history, and degraded her to the level of a vulgar, vain, tawdry woman.

All lovers of truth, justice and religion have a right to protest, as we now do.

The Sacristy had many valuable vestments, but not equal to those of Seville. But it contains relics not easy to be seen elsewhere.

We saw here a piece of a bone of the Virgin Mother, and one of St. Catherine, St. Anthony, St. Augustine, and of many other saints, each not larger than a finger nail.

Here also was a drop of the blood of Christ, on a coarse cloth. Each relic was set in gold, like a precious gem, and covered with a glass. They were then arranged upon a large gold cross, about four feet high, which with all the relics were presented by Pope Clement VII. This grand cross is brought forth in procession on high days, and is worshiped like any other idol.

This cathedral has one picture which is a precious gem, kept veiled from sight except on special occasions. It is a Magdalen, in the Sacristy, by Leonardo da Vinci, a sweet, holy face, full of deep emotion, where repentance and faith beam from her upturned eyes. It is a face more beautiful than that of Mona Lisa by the same artist. The common fame that even the Roman Church has fastened upon the Magdalen is a cruel slander, without warrant of Scripture; but here Leonardo has portrayed her as a pure and holy woman, with no shadow of earthly taint.

THE CID

We cannot leave Burgos without doing honor to the immortal Cid, the very Achilles of all the Spanish heroes. For eight centuries his exploits have been the theme of ballad and song, which are even now sung in every cottage of Castile. He was not a myth, as it has been sometimes represented. His real name was Don Rodrigo Diaz. No picture of Burgos would be complete if this central figure was missing, for here was his home; here he was married; here he dictated terms to princes; here he sleeps in glory among his admiring countrymen. Under St. Ferdinand, the liberator from the yoke of the Moors, the Cid was the champion of the kingdom and of Christians, and as such, often in single combat, decided the issue of battle and the fate of the kingdom. Moors and Jews were his especial hatred. His exploits against infidels and dragons, as told in story and song, partake of the marvelous. Having killed Count Loanzo, the first knight and nobleman of the kingdom, to avenge an insult to his aged father, he was ordered, according to the custom of the times, to make recompense by marrying the daughter of the knight he had slain, and thereafter Xemina became his faithful companion in all his expeditions. After having been treated with neglect and ingratitude by his king, he gathered a band of warriors of kindred spirit, and with them he wrested the whole province of Valencia from the Moors, and established himself as ruler, and there he died in 1091. His body was brought from thence, cased in mail, sitting upright on his favorite horse, Babieca, and was placed in a chapel near Burgos crowned on a throne, with his sword, Tisona, in his hand. A presumptuous Jew having touched his beard as he sat grim in death, the dead warrior raised his mailed arm and knocked the intruder down, whereupon it became necessary to bury him. His bones now rest in a glass case in the town hall of Burgos, with those of his beautiful wife.

In the Cathedral of Burgos, in the sacristy, fastened high up on the wall, is a decaying iron-bound coffer, about five feet square, which has this history:

The Cid, being in want of ready money, persuaded the Jewish bankers that this chest was full of gold, and he pledged it as security for a loan of six hundred marks. It was found filled with sand.

To his honor it must be said he afterward redeemed his pledge.

The ballads of a people probably have more influence upon the character of a nation than any other one influence. For this reason the Cid has done more to mould Spanish character than any man in its history. His religious fanaticism, his knightly valor, his haughty courage, his proud, imperious spirit, breathed through song and ballad, his romantic adventures, read in every home in Spain, where little else is read, are impressing the national character to this day. The songs we sing in childhood are watchwords through our life.

THE PYRENEES.

AT Burgos we are about 150 miles from Irun, where we leave Spain for France. The road rises gradually for 100 miles, until we come upon the Pyrenees, with their lofty peaks around us covered with snow. It is a grand ride through them. We wind up their sides, creep along the face of precipices, make our way into one valley, follow it up until there is no way around, out or over the lofty heights; then we plunge by a tunnel into the very bowels of the mountains, and emerge into another valley. And so we proceed from one to another for fifty miles. The mountains are cold, desolate and barren, but the valleys are beautiful pictures of green verdure, watered by little streams from the hills. As we skirt along the high precipices overhanging these valleys we see far below us the white roads winding through them like lines of chalk, and the narrow, well-trodden sheep paths crossing the opposite mountains in every direction. Thus we passed on through valley after valley, through tunnel after tunnel, just at·sunset, when a peculiar purple light rested on the eastern side of the valleys, glowing with a crimson radiance on the snow-clad tops, or fringing the clouds, which often rolled around their summits. One valley, called Urema, seemed a little paradise, glowing in living green far below us. White, snow-clad mountains piercing the clouds stood sentinels around it on every side, with flowers, bloom, and verdure at their base. At a place called Ormaiztequy we pass, on a grand viaduct of solid masonry, a marvel of engineering skill, hundreds of feet high, from one side of the valley to the other, and at Villareal we pass under a mountain by a tunnel miles in extent.

We are now among the valleys and lofty peaks of this chain of mountains, which are the bulwark of Spain, and isolate it from Europe. They can be distinctly traced as a chain from the Atlantic Ocean into Tartary. When looked at from a distance, as from Montserrat, the chain appears like a vast sea of mountain peaks rising like billows on the stormy ocean, without any order, but in fact they constitute two distinct chains of mountains, from 15 to 30 miles apart, stretching from the sea to the ocean. Many of the peaks are over 11,000 feet high.

There are numerous passes from north to south, but few that can be traversed by wheels. They abound in beautiful valleys, hot and medicinal springs, rare woods and excellent iron ore, wild game and fish.

The southern slope, on the side of Spain, is rough

and precipitous, while the northern front falls off more gradually, with terraces and table lands, into French territory, where there are numerous spas and beautiful healthful resorts for invalids.

The Spanish Pyrenees, both as to cultivation and the habits and manners of the people, remain in the same primitive state in which they were centuries ago.

LOYOLA.

About fifteen miles west of Villa Real, among the mountains, lies the little town of Aspeytea, distinguished only as the birth-place of Ignatius Loyola, who was born in 1491.

After the battle of Pampeluna, in 1515, he retired here desperately wounded, and remained a long time fluttering between life and death, until St. Peter, having pity upon him, descended and healed him. Here, inclosing the very room where he was born, and where he lay so long ill, royal hands have erected a monastery to his memory.

In July every summer a grand pilgrimage is made from all parts of Spain to this shrine, to do honor to this man whose influence has cursed this country for centuries, whose order was annulled by the Pope in 1773, and banished from Spain in 1769. Yet the influence of the Jesuits—an order not of priests only, but one that unites monastic devotion with military discipline and courtly diplomacy—is everywhere felt in Spain. As the most subtle and efficient agency for the propagation and conservation of the Roman Catholic faith, this order is justly appreciated. The deeds of self-sacrificing devotion which they have accomplished in many heathen lands are among the most splendid examples of what the human mind, fired by a tireless enthusiasm, can accomplish. Witness the labors of Francis Xavier in India and Japan, the heroic life and tragic death of Lalemant and Brebœuf and other Jesuit missionaries among the Indians of Canada.

The lives of these men is a romance of devotion to their idea of duty exceeded only by that of St. Paul; and yet a system must be judged by its principles and their effects as worked out on the large scale and through long periods of time, and not from a few solitary examples, however brilliant. Viewed in this light, the order of Loyola would appear far different from what it would if Francis Xavier is taken as a fair exponent of its character. The object of the Order of Jesus was to unite *spiritual and temporal power*, and to perpetuate the Papacy as a *ruling system*, not as a religion. Their principle of action was that " the end justifies the means;" that "faith need not be observed toward heretics;" in other words, that truth and justice, right and wrong, were variable principles, and they the self-constituted judges of their application. Such an assumption, cherished by any order of men, will invariably dry up the better sympathies of their nature, render them subtle, selfish and cruel, and will sap the foundation of all confidence between man and man.

Such has been the history of the Order of Jesus wherever they have gained a foothold. They have been a dark, crafty element of discord in Church and State, despite individual instances of sublime heroism in many of its members.

In forming our judgment of this order, we should consider the *means* used by them. They used the religious sentiment of men to gain ascendancy over their minds. They persuaded the people not to think, not to reason, not to read; they taught that souls would be saved by implicit obedience only. They laid hold, with a worldly policy upon all human means of moving and holding the minds of men. They built fine churches and schools; sent forth missionaries; mingled in courts; sought secular power; united the characteristics of priest and courtier. This deep, crafty policy of saving men's souls for them, of thinking and acting for them, has had and does have its effect in Spain more than in any other country. It falls in with the indolent and superstitious character of the people. You will see in all parts of Spain the black cloak and broad-brimmed hat, and the wary, crafty features of the courtier priest underneath.

Loyola died July 31, 1556, at the age of sixty-three years, and was made a saint about 100 years afterward, and thus we have the spectacle of one infallible Pope suppressing the order of Loyola as dangerous and wicked, and another pope, equally infallible, declaring him a saint.

We now descend the northern slope of the Pyrenees through many romantic passes, which are the key to Spain, and which were fought for by Wellington and Napoleon. We are now in one of the Basque Provinces, which are so full of interest to the ethnologist. Here we find a people whose origin and language are pre-historic.

Irun is the last town on the frontier. The River Bidassoa is the boundary line between France and Spain. As we cross this on a fine iron bridge, we notice far below us a small island in the river, which has been the scene of many important events. It is called the Isle of Conference. It is neutral ground, and as such the sovereigns of France and Spain have made this the place of their mutual negotiations for many centuries. It was at Bayonne, a few miles from here, that Catharine de Medicis, of France, and the Duke of Alva, representing Philip II. of Spain, met and planned the Massacre of St. Bartholomew, which was so successfully carried out that 30,000 Protestants were slaughtered on the 24th and 25th days of August, 1572. This deed of blood, which horrified the rest of the civilized world, was approved by the Pope, who ordered a general thanksgiving to God, whose gospel of love, peace and good-will to men had been so signally illustrated thereby.

The journey across France from Bayonne to Marseilles will bring us to our starting place.

BAYONNE

is situated on the Adour and the Nive, near the sea, has a good harbor, docks and numerous manufactories. Here we begin to feel the pulses of business life, in strange contrast with the deadness on the other side of the Pyrenees. The Adour runs through the town, and is crossed by massive bridges. The streets are wide, and open into large and well-built squares. The railroad to Toulouse follows up the Adour to the East. On every hand the people are at work in the fields; cows are yoked to carts and plows; the farming instruments are not so rude as those used in Spain. On our right hand all the way across the kingdom tower the Pyrenees. We pass through Pau, situate on a high plateau 250 feet above the Gave de Pau, with a beautiful green valley along its banks. On this plateau are situated the hotels looking down on the river and valley, and beyond it a few miles, lie a line of low blue mountains, and beyond them to the South the snow-clad Pyrenees, which stretch away to the East in peaks, cones and serrated ridges as far as the eye can reach. The railroad winds along the river, continually ascending, until we strike a spur of the Pyrenees at a point where the river breaks through, and then we rise in a few miles 600 feet, and emerge into an upland valley with mountain tops all around and the snow-capped Pyrenees from a distance looking into it. This is the village of

LOURDES,

which has so recently been added to the already long array of shrines made holy by the miraculous presence of the Virgin. Upon a hill just out of the village is a splendid new church erected over the place where the Virgin mother appeared to a peasant girl in 1858. The poor people, out of curiosity, began to flock to the place, and still the wonder grew, until in a few weeks 150,000 persons had come to see it. The authorities at last forbade the assemblage as a nuisance. The Bishop of Tarbes thought better of it. A holy shrine in any man's bishopric is not to be despised. Every pilgrim leaves a certain amount of money. The bishop declared the miracle veritable.

Here now come pilgrims from all parts of the world. At this time a pilgrimage under the direction of a distinguished English nobleman, is on its way to the shrine, said to be undertaken for the purpose of enlisting the sympathies of the Virgin in behalf of England in her difficulties with Ireland.

Why is it that none of these holy places are found in Protestant countries? Is it because Catholics would be ashamed to defend them in the face of Protestants, or is it that the Virgin will not vouchsafe her presence among Protestants? But why should she not use her power to convert unbelievers? Is not this the province of miracles? Would not all Protestants be persuaded could they witness a veritable miracle? Is it not a fact that the alleged miracles always happen among ignorant, superstitious people, liable to excitement and deception? Have they ever been performed among the more matter-of-fact people of Germany, England, Scotland, and the United States?

LANGUEDOC.

In pursuing our journey to Toulouse, the capital of ancient Languedoc, we strike the head waters of the Garonne, and pursue its beautiful valley north-east through a rich and well-cultivated country. Languedoc was the ancient name for a number of departments in France with more modern names which lie north of the Pyrenees and west of the Rhone. Its capital was Toulouse, which is a fine city, with 130,000 inhabitants, situated on the River Garonne, which is crossed by a magnificent bridge, 810 feet long and 72 feet wide. It is surrounded by a rich agricultural district, and has a large trade for an inland town. It is well built, with many large squares, and is more emphatically a French city than other cities farther north, which are more frequented by foreigners. Here was born Henry IV of France.

Languedoc has a mournful history. At the beginning of the thirteenth century it was one of the most fertile, sunny, happy parts of France until the Inquisition laid its bloody hand upon it, scathed it with fire and deluged it with blood in the name of religion.

It was the land of poetry and song, of elegance and freedom, the home of the Troubadour. Count Bayard VI was then prince. By their association with Barcelona and other cities recently Moorish, and with Jews and Arabs in the seaports, the people came to cherish tolerance in religious opinions, and here at last grew up the heresy of denying the supremacy of the Pope, the authority of the priesthood, the efficacy of prayer for the dead, and the existence of purgatory. They reviled the enormities of the priests in their ballads. They were rich, joyous, worldly, happy. Their beautiful land, their wealth, their happy, careless life, excited the envy of that great high priest of the Inquisition, Dominic Guzman. He could not endure either their loose ballads or their heresy, and at last, under the authority of Pope Innocent III, he began to preach the extermination of the Albigenses, so called from Alby, a city of Languedoc. Here the Inquisition was first established, to hunt out and try heretics by torture and death. Its administration was committed to the fanatical Castilian, Dominic.

It did not succeed in extirpating the heresy, and then the famous crusade against the Albigenses was preached and prosecuted by the Church, from 1208 to 1220. This crusade was the most noted, bloody, and disgraceful event of the thirteenth century. It called together an army composed of rude northern knights, and of the wild, reckless spirits of the age led by Simon de Montfort, thirsting for blood and plunder. Allured by the hope of sacking the beautiful and rich cities of Southern France, they came in hordes, like vultures to the prey, and for twelve years this war was carried on with the most savage ferocity under the authority of the

Pope. The human tigers reveled in blood. It was a crusade without the peril of a long journey to Palestine. It was a rich land to plunder; it was a happy, joyous clime in which to revel; it was an opportunity to gratify all the brutal passions of a brutal age, under the sanction of religion and with the promise of Paradise. The Vicar of the meek and loving Christ, from his throne in the Vatican, said in his commission: "You shall ravage every field; you shall slay every human being. Strike and spare not. The measure of their iniquity is full and the blessing of the Church is on your heads."

This beautiful, sunny land of the Troubadour was soon a smoking ruin. The savage hordes of foreign invaders sacked the cities, slaughtered women and children, until these missionaries of the Mother Church had murdered one-half of the people, and until the friar Dominic himself could no longer endure the sight of the flowing blood which reddened all her rivers and her sunny plains. This is said to have been the first essay the Church made to sustain its supremacy by force of arms against Christians. Hitherto pagans and infidels only had felt the constraining influence of the Christian sword, but now and hereafter the heretic was to try its restraining power, and from this date the Inquisition took its rise. Its tortures and its fires were for ages afterward to be the agents of persuasion instead of reason and love. In this war, by one assault on Beziers, 20,000 persons were destroyed in cold blood for having given protection to fugitives. The Abbot of Cetaux was present with the commission and as the representative of the Pope. The soldiers were in doubt how to distinguish, in their indiscriminate slaughter, the heretics from the believers. The Bishop in his holy zeal solved the difficulty by saying, "Slay them all. The Lord will know his own." This bishop gave an account of the slaughter to the Pope, and regretted he had been able to slay only 20,000. In this Albigensian war 250,000 lives were offered up as a holocaust to the God of love, as a mark of the zeal and loyalty of his vicegerent on the throne of the Vatican.

Oh, religion, what crimes have been done in thy name!

Our journey takes us through Castelnaudary, Carcassonne, and Beziers, all places of note in this crusade, and which suffered terribly at the hands of the fierce bigot, Simon de Montfort.

We pass the cities of Narbonne, Cette, Nismes, all of which are places of interest, but which we cannot stop to describe. At Tarrascon we cross the Rhone, and are soon at our starting place, the City of Marseilles, and our journey from the Pyrenees to the Pillars of Hercules is ended.

It may appear as if we had been seeking every

opportunity to show the dark and tragic deeds done in the name of religion, but the truth is that the Catholic religion has had a more complete sway over the human mind in Spain than in any other country on the globe, not excepting Italy. It has allied itself with government, and for carrying out its policy for the elevation and salvation of the human mind it has here always had the arm of civil power to enforce its behests, and has thus had a fair test for centuries with every human resource at its disposal.

As its marked deeds and triumphs come out on the page of history, from age to age, as place after place recalls them in our travels, does not truth and justice to principle demand that these deeds, the outcome of a great, the greatest ecclesiastical polity of the world, should be fairly stated?

Puritanism must be responsible for persecution of witchcraft, and explain it as best it can; Calvin for the death of Servetus; Mohammedanism for polygamy; and Romanism for the Inquisition, for St. Bartholomew's day, for the massacre of the Albigenses, and for Jesuitism and Mariolatry. After centuries of trial it is fair to judge every system of religion by its effects. The divine rule must be applied: "By their fruits ye shall know them." On this principle compare England and Spain, Ireland and Scotland, New England and the South American States, any Protestant with any Catholic country.

With these reflections and apologies we bid farewell to Spain, the land of the past. Poor, proud, haughty, ignorant, living on her past glories, which she wraps around her nakedness, as one of her poverty-stricken hidalgos, glorying in his lofty lineage, draws his ancient cloak around his lank limbs and tattered garments, and persuades himself that he is still one of the grand old knights of other days.

But the days of her humiliation will end. When a pure, benign Christian religion shall be taught by her priesthood; when superstition shall lose its sway; when education shall elevate the people, and a free liberal government shall extend its shield of protection over them; when the colors of its patriots like Castelar shall be crowned with success, then will Spain again resume her place among the great nations of the earth with all her ancient prestige and glory.

THE END.

www.ingramcontent.com/pod-product-compliance
Lightning Source LLC
Chambersburg PA
CBHW021406230426
43666CB00006B/653